New Discoveries About VEDIC SARASVATĪ

By

Dr. Ravi Prakash Arya

AMAZON BOOKS, USA

In association with

INDIAN FOUNDATION FOR VEDIC SCIENCE

H.O.1051, Sector-1, Rohtak-124001, Haryana, India

Delhi Contact Ph. Nos : 09313033917; 09650183260

Emails : vedicscience@hotmail.com; vedicscience@rediffmail.com

Website : www.vedicscience.net

Fourth Edition

Kali era: 5015 (c. 2014)
Kalpa era: 1,97,29,49,115
Brahma era: 15,50,21,97,9,49,115

ISBN No. 81-87710-69-1

Contents

Foreword

It gives me a great pleasure that the much-awaited work on the legendary Vedic Sarasvatī is before the readers and the scholars. The author has for the first time presented a systematic study of various flows of Sarasvatī in various phases right from the Vedic down to the *Mahābhārata* period as described in the vast Vedic and post-Vedic literature. In fact, such an academic study of Sarasvatī as the present one has long been a desideratum. Though there are many publications available in the market on Sarasvatī, but they all have been written with the assumptions that modern day tracks of Mārkaṇḍā and Ghaggar represent the remnants of old Vedic Sarasvatī. This type of research gives a wrong information about the various flows of Sarasvatī as depicted in the Vedic and Paurāṇika literature. With the publication of the present title 'New Discoveries about Vedic Sarasvatī' a long felt ardent need has been fulfilled. Much to the satisfaction of the readers and the scholars of Vedas, History and Archaeology, the present work is most original one accomplished in a recent decade. This work would certainly set aside the various unfounded notions and ill-conceived assumptions, flimsy suppositions regarding the various origins and flows of perennial Vedic Sarasvatī. This work would help the archaeologists, historians and other scholars interested in the study of Vedic Sarasvatī to formulate their views and theories on the origin and evolution of Vedic Sarasvatī as per the description of Sarasvatī available in the Vedic and post-Vedic Sanskrit literature. Since Sarasvatī is purely a Vedic concept and as such no one has the moral right to make surmises and postulate imaginary theories without their assumptions being supported by the Vedic and Paurāṇika records. It's really painful when some scholars try to read their preconceived notions and project their own views in the Vedas and Purāṇas. In fact, instead of resorting to such tactics, they should preferably try to confirm whether their findings are vindicated by the Vedic and Paurāṇika views. It is fervently hoped that the publication of the present volume would help stop further speculations regarding Sarasvatī and help the readers and scholars develop a view of Vedic Sarasvatī in right and proper perspective.

Here it may also be pointed out that Vedic culture flourished on the banks of Sarasvatī. The location of lost Sarasvatī will determine the origin of Vedic culture. The foreigners who are hell bent to locate Vedic culture outside India, have failed miserably in their vain attempts to locate Sarasvatī outside India in central Asia. On the other hand, modern researches on Sarasvatī have proved beyond any shadow of a doubt that the much talked about Sarasvatī used to flow in India.

Dr. Ravi Prakash Arya
114-Akash, DRDO Complex
Lucknow Road, Timarpur
Delhi-110054 (India)
Ph. +91 9313033917; +91 9650183260
vedicscience@hotmail.com
vedicscience@rediffmail.com
www.vedascience.com

Introduction

Sarasvatī is the perennial river of Bhārata. It is the very soul of Indian culture and thickly embedded in the entire fabric of Indian psyche. In fact, Sarasvatī and Indian culture both are interwoven. The origin of this great perennial culture of the world known as Vedic culture owes its origin to the very origin of Sarasvatī. But the question of the place of the origin of Sarasvatī is perplexing and vexing the scholars since the last quarter of 19th century. Scholars coming from various disciplines have had their say as to the various origins of Sarasvatī basing their arguments on various evidence ranging from Sanskrit literature to the LANDSAT imagery and other modest techniques of research.

However, most of the studies carried out so far are based either on the interpretation of LANDSAT imagery or field verifications in the Indian part of the desert or the archaeological remains associated with old river courses. Literary sources have though been taken into account by many scholars, but they are mainly confined to describing the greatness and various epithets of the mighty Sarasvatī or at the most they try to find some literary evidence in support of their postulations and conjectures formulated on the basis of findings from archaeological excavations and LANDSAT imagery regarding the origin of Sarasvatī. For instance, the evidences from archaeological remains associated with old river courses have suggested that a major river stemming mainly from the same source as the present Sutlej flowed through northern Rajasthan, Bahawalpur and Sind to the south-east of the present course of the Sutlej and Indus in the third millennium BC (Allchin Goudie and Hegde, 1987). It is also suggested that the river used to flow through Raini and Wahind rivers and then through eastern Nara and Hakra in the

Sind province of Pakistan to the Rann of Kutch (Oldham 1893; Wadia 1938; Ali 1942; Stein 1942; Krishan 1960; Wilhelmy, 1969). The evidence gathered from the interpretation of aerial photographs and LANDSAT imagery tends to prove that the Sarasvatī formerly used to flow through a more easterly course in the Rajasthan part of the desert when the Luni river was one of its tributaries. Subsequently, the river shifted its course to the west several times and finally severed its link with the Luni (Ghose et al, 1978). The evidence from the aforementioned sources further leads to prove that when the river severed its link from Luni and shifted westward, it didn't occupy the Raini-Wahind-Nara- Hakra course in Pakistan.

But the main problem is that none of the scholars has so far been able to direct his archaeological or other studies in the light of numerous and varied information lying scattered in the vast Vedic and post-Vedic literature on the various phases of existence of Sarasvatī. In fact the vast and extensive informative data on various phases of existence of Sarasvatī has mixed up in such a manner that it becomes very difficult for a lay scholar, who is not well-acquainted with the Vedic dicta to systematically arrange and consolidate the data phase-wise and thereby to present an integrated account of the origin and flow of Sarasvatī during various phases ranging from Vedic down to the age of *Mahābhārata* (c.3138 BC.) and afterwards.

Origin of Sarasvatī in the Vedic Phase

The first origin of Sarasvatī in the Vedic phase goes with the very origin of waters on the earth and as such Sarasvatī is described in the Vedas as owing its origin to clouds. The Ṛgvedic seer Vasiṣṭha has clearly indicated in his observations that celestial *Parvatas* were the source of origin of Sarasvatī:

ā no divo bṛhataḥ parvatādā, sarasvatī yajatāgantu yajñam
havaṁ devi jujuṣāṇā ghṛtācī,śagmo no vācamuśatī śṛṇot

From the great celestial *parvata* (cloud), Sarasvatī flows

towards the *yañīya* site. It hears the voice of a person who offers the oblation of *ghṛta* or clarified butter with the desire to receive it.'

Here the use of the phrase *divaḥ Parvata* clearly suggests that the celestial *parvata* here is not the terrestrial mountain but the cloud in the sky.

The fact is that *parvata* or its synonyms have never been used for mountains in the earlier Vedic language. They always signified clouds. Yāska (*Nirukta*: 1.20) observed in this connection as follows:

giriṣṭhā giristhāyī giriḥ parvataḥ samudgīrṇo bhavati parvavān parvataḥ parva punaḥ pṛṇāteḥ prīṇātaṁ vārdhmāsa parva devānasmin prīṇantīti ut prakṛtītarat sandhi sāmānyāt meghasthāyī megho'pi giriretasmādeva

Giri is known as *parvata* (mountain) since it stands to protrude the surface of the earth. It is called as *Parvata*, because it is constituted of ranges of hills. It adds to the happiness of the living beings on the earth by providing water. These qualities are also discernible in the clouds, so a cloud, too, is called *giri*.

The author of the present lines has already established at several places that Vedic dicta formed in the cultural, geographical or geological or scientific background prevalent by that time. The Indian culture is not 3,4 or10 thousand years old as is often considered. In fact, this great perennial culture, as it is known from its chronology available in the *Purāṇas* and its era retained in the *Saṁkalpa pāṭhas*, is older than the oldest Himalayas. This culture flourished around 197 crore years ago when there were no mountains visible on the earth. So it was natural that Vedic people had no mountains to denote them by the term *parvata*. In the light of the above discussion, the oft-repeated Ṛgvedic *Mantra* revealed to the Vasiṣṭha

ekā cetat sarasvatī nadīnām śuciryatī
giribhya ā samudrāt. (7.95.2)

cannot be taken for Sarasvatī as flowing from mountains to the sea, rather it would be taken to mean Sarasvatī flowing from clouds to sea.

Brahmanic Origin of Sarasvatī

The second origin of Sarasvatī belongs to the *Brāhmaṇic* phase, during which it was known to have originated from *Plakṣa Prasravaṇa.* This fact has been corroborated by several Puranic traditions also. *Plakṣa Prasravaṇa* of Brāhmaṇic period points out Sarasvatī oozing or thawing out of the Himalayas, the glaciated region. There are clear cut indications in the tradition of the *Skand Purāṇa* (7.30.41) that Sarasvatī having approached the glaciers flowed on the earth through *Plakṣa.* The approach of Sarasvatī to glaciers was its precipitation in the form of snowflakes from clouds and its flow in the form of waters on the earth has been assigned to place called *Plakṣa.* In fact, *Plakṣa* may be recalled as the place of origin of Sarasvatī during the period when the present day Himalayan region witnessed the first ever glaciation since the origin of the earth.

Origin of Sarasvatī from *Plakṣa* is also registered in the memories of other *Purāṇas,* e.g. according to *Vāmana Purāṇa* (3-4), Perennial Sarasvatī originated from *Plakṣa* tree.

plakṣa vṛkṣāt samudbhūtā saricchreṣṭhā sanātanī

In *Bṛhannāradīya Purāṇa* (64-17) also Sarasvatī has been described as *Plakṣa Jātā,* i.e. originated from *Plakṣa.*

mārkaṇḍeyena muninā saṁtaptaṁ paramaṁ tapaḥ
tatra- tatra samāyātā plakṣajātā sarasvatī

In *Tāṇḍya Brāhmaṇa* (25.10.16) the distance between the place of drying up (*Vinaśana*) and point of rising of Sarasvatī has been measured as 44 *Āśvins.*

catuścatvāriṁśadāśvināni sarasvatyā vinaśanāt plakṣaḥ prāsravaṇaḥ

"The distance between Plakṣa and *Vinaśana* is as long as 44 *Āśvins.*"

Now the main question is to ascertain the nature of *Plakṣ a*, whether it was the name of a place or of a tree as mentioned in several books. If it was the name of a place, the probem is where and how to locate it?

Plakṣa, in fact, was the name of a place, perhaps conspicuous with the presence of *Plakṣa* trees. One should not get oneself confused with *Plakṣa* as tree or place. *Plakṣa* as tree is often known in vernaculars as Pilakhana or a fig tree. It is known in botanical terms as *ficus religiosa*. Due to rising of Sarasvatī from a place of *Plakṣa* trees. *Plakṣa* was attached a religious fervour and the tree is considered to be holy. Such a place, which was conspicuous with *Plakṣa* tree is Pilakhua in western UP. This place is located near Hapur and Garhgaṅgā. Pilakhua is obviously named after Pilakhana, a corrupt form of *Plakṣa*. Now we shall see whether *Plakṣa* can be situated at modern Pilakhua as per literary records of Vedas, *Purāṇas* or Epics.

1). In this regard, a reference of *Vāmana Purāṇa* (3-4) may be cited. Accordingly, Sarasvatī after crossing thousands of stones entered the Dvaitavana.

saiṣā śailasahasrāṇi vidārya ca mahā nadī
praviṣṭā puṇyatoyaiṣā vanaṁ daivatamiti śrutam

N.L Dey has located the area of Dvaitavana near about Deoband in modern UP which is 50 miles north of Meerut or ancient *Marudhanvan* (*Āraṇyaka Parva* 243.21:295. 8:296.40 BORI, Poona)

2). King Yudhiṣṭhira started from Kurujāṅgala towards the north on the bank of river Sarasvatī in search of some thick forest full of roots and fruits after sometime he entered Dvaitavana.

There is also a reference of Pāṇḍvas proceeding towards Sarasvatī to the north of Marudhanvan (Modern Meerut) Thus it is clear from the above-cited references that route of Sarasvatī was once via or close to the area of Deoband located to the north of Marudhanvan (Meerut)

3). Next is the location of Kāmyaka vana. According to Chapter 244 of Āryaṇyaka Parva, Kāmyaka vana was there almost in Marudeśa. Here it may be clarified that Marudeśa i.e. Marusthal or desert land was not far from Hastinapur. From the north of Kāmyakavana began the forests of Himalayas. Thus the location of Dvaitavana on the banks of Sarasvatī and closeness of Dvaitavana and Kāmyakavana to the Himalayan hills and forests respectively reveals that Sarasvatī in Brāhmaṇic period flowed through UP and *Plakṣa* was nothing but the modern Pilakhua. As per the author of *Geography of Mahābhārata* (P.213), from Plakṣa Prasravaṇa; Iśānudhyāsī tīrtha was at a distance of about half a mile, i.e. the name of tīrtha is indicative of Śiva temple. It can also be located in or around Pilakhua.

4). *Mahābhārata* (*Vanaparva*: 8.3-84) enumerates *Plakṣa* in the list of 113 *tīrthas* lying in Kuru region. Kuru region is identified with modern regions of Thaneshwar, Delhi, Meerut and Bijnor between Sarasvatī and Gaṅgā rivers having its capital at Hastinapur (near modern Bijnor). (*Geographical Horizon of Mahābhārata* P.137). *Jain Ādi Purāṇa* (16.193) also locates Kurujāṅgala in between Sarasvatī and Gaṅgā.

Vanaparva of *Mahābhārata* enumerates Gaṅgā-Sarasvatī Saṅgam (84.38) as one of the *tīrthas* located in Kuru regions. This makes it explicitly clear that Sarasvatī and Gaṅgā must be joining each other at some place in Kuru region and meeting place of Gaṅgā and Sarasvatī in the Kuru region can be none other but the area around Garhgaṅgā and Pilakhua in western UP.

5) While recounting *Plakṣa* as the tīrtha of Kurukshetra, it is told that Sarasvatī originated from a Bamboo near Saugandhika Vana which has also been identified near Mandākinī river of Garhwal hills of UP. Here it may not be odd to relate a folk tale of Bhutias of Mana village lying in the Garhwal region of UP. The folk tradition of the villagers remembers the origin of Sarasvatī in the region of Mana pass at an altitude of 18,400 feet above sea level. This pass is

surrounded by high peaks covered with a huge mass of snow and ice and lies on the old trade route along Indo Tibetan border to Garhwal region of UP. From Mana Pass to Mana village, Sarasvatī covers a distance of 45 kms. In the high altitude regions of the Himalayas. The altitude varies from 11,000 feet at Keshava Prayāg (the Meeting Point of Sarasvatī and Alaknandā) more than 18,000 feet at the origin. As per folk tale, the river goes down *Pātāl Loka* from Bhima Bridge, leaving a small stream to meet Alaknandā. The rest of river reappears at Prayāg rāj to form the Triveṇī. The fact is that before its junction with Alaknandā at Keshav Prayāg, the Sarasvatī falls in a deep and narrow gorge below Bhima Bridge, which is a rock bridge reportedly built by one of the five famous Pāṇḍva brothers Bhima during 12 years long wandering period. The gorge is 150 to 200 feet deep. The river Sarasvatī emerges from gorge with sound and fury in white caps and meets Alaknandā to form Keshav Prayāg.

Thus from the local tradition of folk tales also it is crystal clear that *Plakṣa* was a place below glaciated region and during Brāhmaṇic period most probably it was Pilakhua situated on the route of Gaṅgā.

6) As pointed out above, according to *Tāṇḍya Brāhmaṇa* (25.10.1-23) the distance from *Vinaśana* to Plakṣa Prasravaṇa is 44 *Āśvins.* At the same distance from *Plakṣa* is situated *Svarga loka.* So people who want to go to *Svarga loka* take a journey alongwith the stream of Sarasvatī.

catuścatvāriṁśadāśvināni sarasvatyā vinaśanāt plakṣaḥ prāsravaṇaḥ tāvaditaḥ savargo lokaḥ sarasvatī sammitena adhvanā savargaṁ lokaṁ yanti.

Here it may be known to the scholars and others that *Svarga loka* in the Sanskrit language implies to the northern region of Garhwal area of Mandākinī river in upper Himalayan ranges. Hence as per reference of *Tāṇḍya Brāhmaṇa* cited above *Plakṣa* was situated at equidistant from *Vinaśana* and Garhwal Himalayan region. The *Yajikās* used to go to *Svarga loka* along with the stream of Sarasvatī. Here it may be clarified that *Plakṣa* was not located on the hilly terrain, rather it was located in plains.

Sarasvatī's track from Garhwal region down to *Plakṣa*, clearly points out that Pilakhua can only be the exact location of *Plakṣa*.

Here it may also be given to understand that in Brāhmaṇic period Sarasvatī never terminated at western sea, rather it terminated at *Vinaśana* itself around 44 *Āśvins* from *Plakṣa*. This fact also points out that in Brāhmaṇic period Sarasvatī may not have been a big river as was the case in the later period. In fact, the Brāhmaṇic period may be considered as the glaciated period. As per modern Geologists in Triassic period i.e. 22 crore years ago northern hemisphere consisting of the present-day Europe was still a desert, but the southern hemisphere consisting of Indian continent was covered with snow. The memory of this type of glaciation still exists in the memory of the *Purāṇas*. Thus during this Brāhmaṇic phase, Sarasvatī had a small track to flow.

Sarasvatī's flow till western sea is described in the *Skand Purāṇa* in the context of draining the *Vaḍvānala* (7.33.40-41) to the western sea at Prabhāsa Pāṭan. *Vaḍvāgni* was nothing else but the submarine volcanic activities of Mānas sara or the Tethys sea. It is well known that Himalayan ranges of mountains formed from volcanoes caused by plate-tectonic upheavals at the submarine level of Mānas sea. Due to volcanic activities at the submarine level of Mānas sara, the upliftment of the bottom began to take place. This upliftment caused the dewatering of the sea. This outflow of uplifted Mānas sara drained towards the western sea at Prabhāsa Pāṭan was called as Sarasvatī. This period goes back to the age of the first phase of formation of the Himalayan ranges. Himalayan ranges began to form in Eocene period i.e. around 7 crore years ago, but according to Indian tradition, the Himalayan ranges began to form in the beginning of *Vaivasvata Manvantara*. i.e. 12 crore years ago. We also meet some references in the *Purāṇas* that describe the origin of Sarasvatī from the upper Himalayan ranges. According to the tradition of *Matsya Purāṇa* (121.64-65), Sarasvatī and Jyotiṣmatī rivers flowing towards western and eastern seas respectively issue from *Sarpa* or *Nāga* lake situated at the back of Hemakūṭa.

parasprena dviguṇā dharmataḥ kāmato'rthataḥ
hemakūṭasya pṛṣṭhe tu sarpāṇāṁ tatsaraḥ smṛtaḥ-64
sarasvatī prabhavati tasmājjyotiṣmati tu yā
avaghāḍhe hyubhayataḥ samudrau pūrvapaścimau.-65

Vāyu Purāṇa (*Gaṅgā Avtāra-Varṇana*-Chp. 47) depicts the same fact only with a few minor variations, e.g. *Sarpa* or *Nāga* lake has been mentioned as Śyanā lake and Sarasvatī has been mentioned as Manasvinī.

In the reference given above, Hemakūṭa is modern Kailāśa range (Ali: 1973) and the Sarpa lake or Śyanā lake at the back of Kailash, according to Ali, is the lake Nak Tso which with the Pangong Tso forms an extensive water sheet which join the Shyok at its southeastern bend and then combined waters flow towards the western sea (Ali, P.70-71)

Today also we find two river systems Sindhu and Brahmaputra issuing from Mānasarovar lakes i.e. Sindhu from Mānasarovar and Brahmaputra from Rakṣasa Tāla, whereby Sindhu enters into western sea and Brahmaputra in eastern sea. *Matsya Purāṇa* names Sindhu as Manasvinī due to its origin from Mānasarovar. *Vāyu Purāṇa* retains its old name Sarasvatī only. It was caled Sarasvatī because it issued from Mānas sara. Similarly, it was called Manasvinī after the name Mānas. On the other hand, Brahmaputra has been named as Jyotiṣmatī by both, since it flows towards east or the direction of Jyotiṣpur or Prāg-Jyotiṣpur(Assam). Jyotiṣpur or Prāg-Jyotiṣpur is a place where the sun rises first in India.

In fact, Sindhu and Brahmaputra are the two separated streams of one and same Sarasvatī. They are the creation of Himalayan ranges. In the *Nadī Sūkta* of *Ṛgveda* Sindhu and Brhmaputra have not been mentioned, since the Ṛgvedic *Nadī Sūkta* was composed before the origin of Himalayan ranges.

It was after the formation of the upper Himalayan region that the mighty flow of Sarasvatī got separated into two streams, well known in the tradition of *Padma Purāṇa* (5.18; 117-28; 123) and *Skanda Purāṇa* (7.35.26) as Prācī Sarasvatī and Paśćimābhimukhi Sarasvatī which are Sindhu and Brahmaputra respectively. *Mahābhārata Anuśāsana Parva* (134.15) clearly mentions that Sarasvatī originated first of all the rivers:

eṣā sarasvatī puṇyā nadināmuttamā nadi
prathmā sarvasaritāṁ nadi sāgargāminī

The above arguments and the present *śloka* of *Mahābhārata* clearly show that Sarasvatī was the oldest stream, which was later known as the divided stream of the Sindhu and Brahmaputra.

Thus the origin of Sarasvatī after formation of upper Himalayan ranges as a divided stream from lakes variously called in the *Purāṇas* as Mānas lake or Sarpa lake or Nāga lake was known as *Nāégodbheda* (issuing from the upper Himalayan region). *Nāk* literally means *Svarga.* i.e. upper Himalayan region.

Śivodbheda

In the last Himalayan phase, we find the origin of Siwalik hills. In fact, Kailash region was famous as the abode of Śiva (while in the glaciation period it was famous as a *Himvat* region). Later on when the hilly terrain developed at the lower regions of Kailash, that came to be known as flocks of Śiva or *Śivālaka* or Siwalik in the present sense of terms. Siwalik ranges are also known as *Himvatpāda* being the last phase of Himalayas.

With the origin of Siwalik ranges, we find a shift in connection of Sarasvatī from Sindhu or Brahmaputra (Jyotiṣmatī) to Gaṅgā. Its origin also came to be known as Śivodbheda like that of Gaṅgā's fall on the flocks of Śiva from *Svarga.*

The tradition of *Brahma Purāṇa* sheds an ample good light on this fact by way of narrating a story that Sarasvatī owing to the fear of Brahmā's growing love towards her submerged itself into the basin of Gaṅgā. In fact, the eastern region was always known as the *Brāhma* region or *Brahmarṣi deśa* or Burma as is well known today. And northern region as *Śaiva* region. Sarasvatī's fear of growing love of Brahmā clearly indicates the drainage of maximum waters of Sarasvatī towards east through its eastern stream/ channel called Brahmaputra. With the partition of Sarasvatī into Sindhu and Brahmaputra, its downward main flow got abandoned. This fact is revealed in the *Purāṇas* in a figurative manner. The *Purāṇa* narrates the story of Sarasvatī's merging into the basin of Gaṅgā. The tradition of *Brahmavaivarta Purāṇa* also holds the view that Sarasvatī and Gaṅgā had the same origin. The one and the sameness of Gaṅgā and Sarasvatī is also substantiated by a tradition of *Vāmana Purāṇa* (Chap.42) wherein it is ruled that if one takes a dip into the eastern flow of Sarasvatī he gets the benefit of taking a dip into Gaṅgā.

pūrva pravāhe yaḥ snāti gaṅgāsnānaphalaṁ labhet

In fact, in post Siwalik phase eastern flow of Sarasvatī was associated with Gaṅgā only.

The connection between Sarasvatī and Gaṅgā could also be established on the basis of *Plakṣa* (or Pilakhua) as the origin of Sarasvatī during Brāhmaṇic period. Ancient *Plakṣa* or modern Pilakhua being situated at a point close to the basin of Gaṅgā or Garhgaṅgā. Thus the original source of Vedic Sarasvatī (*Plakṣa*) and modern Gaṅgā (Garhgaṅgā) i.e. home of Gaṅgā being close to each other, the third origin of Sarasvatī as Siwalik Sarasvatī, *Śivodbheda* Sarasvatī or lost Sarasvatī and Gaṅgā was recognised as one and same.

Delinking of Sarasvatī from Gaṅgā

The Purāṇic traditions further shed light on the delinking of Sarasvatī from Gaṅgā. *Brahmavaivarta Purāṇa* (Chp. 6.70-71) holds that there arose a dispute between Gaṅgā and Sarasvatī in which both exchange curses leading to a pledge by Gaṅgā to end Sarasvatī's existence. *Purāṇa* tells us that cursed by Gaṅgā to turn black, Sarasvatī descended on the holy place of Bhārata, which undoubtedly is Kurukshetra.

puṇyakṣetre hyājagāma bhārate sā sarasvatī
gaṅgāśāpena kalayā svayaṁ tasthau hareḥ padam.

(*Brahmavaivarta Purāṇa* 2.7.1)

Here Gaṅgā's curse to blacken Sarasvatī clearly reveals the fact that after severing its link with Gaṅgā, Sarasvatī's origin was associated with the place of origin of Yamunā whose water is considered to be of black hue as compared to that of Gaṅgā. Here starts the fourth origin of Sarasvatī.

This fact has also been described by the tradition of *Skanda Purāṇa* (7.33.40-41). As per the tradition, the *Plakṣa* descended on the famous Yamunā tīrtha which was also known as the doorstep to the *Nāk* or heaven, i.e. the upper Himalayas.

etad vai plakṣāvataraṇaṁ yamunātīrthamuttamaṁ
etad vai nākpṛṣṭhasya dvāramāhurmanīṣiṇaḥ

Yamunā also used to flow to the westward sea, till *Mahābhārata* period. It is evident from the *Yātrā parva* of *Mahābhārata* (Chap., verse 3)

kāmyakaṁ nāma dadṛśurvanaṁ munijana priyam
samudragā mahāvegā yamunā yatra pāṇḍava.

Its eastern flow in the form of a small stream also came into being by the time of *Mahābhārata,* as is evident from the story of Vasudeva's wading across the river Yamunā on the day of Kṛṣṇa Janmāṣṭamī in August to carry the Kṛṣṇa to the safe custody of Yaśodharā in Nanda Gāon. Its southern stream had already started drying up at Kurukshetra, except Pṛthudak where Yudhiṣṭhira performed the last rite of his relatives.

After *Mahābhārata* Period the southern stream of Yamunā dried up completely. The excavation in the area of Pṛthudak and others has made it clear that there were a number of cities which were neither destroyed by floods nor by human attacks. Kālibaṅgā is one of such cities which was abandoned during 1300-1400 Kali era or c.1800-1700 BC. as shown by Radiocarbon dating of the material recovered from that city. Below the Harappan citadel of Kalibangan are the remains of the pre-Harappan township which were destroyed around 650 and 800 Kali era i.e. c. 2450 and 2300 BC. This indicates that above cities were abandoned due to shifting of Yamunā's waters from its southward flowing mainstream to the eastward flowing sub-stream (named Kālindī) which came into being already in *Mahābhārata* period i.e. around 45 years before Kali era.

Geographic and sedimentological evidence are also now available to make it clear that southward mainstream and eastward flowing sub-stream were deriving water from one and the same channel.

Thus with the diversion of Yamunā from south to east, its southern track went dry and became as a rain-fed river deriving almost all of its waters from Ādibadri of Sirmaur hills of Ambala district. This diversion caused the absence of the Sarasvatī and seeing this absence, as is had from *Purāṇas*, Mārkaṇḍeya Muni did some efforts to feed its old track with water deriving from a channel (known after his name as Mārkaṇḍā) issuing from Ādibadri of Sirmaur hills

mārkaṇḍeyena muninā saṁtaptaṁ paramaṁ tapaḥ
tatra tatra samāyātā plakṣajātā sarasvatī
sā sabhājya stutā tena muninā dhārmikena ha
saraḥsannihitaṁ plāvya paścimena prasthitā diśam

So Mārkaṇḍā Sarasvatī is the last Sarasvatī or the fifth Sarasvatī in the chain.

1

Rediscovering Vedic Sarasvatī

As already pointed out, much has been discussed and debated since the last quarter of 19th century regarding the various aspects of Sarasvatī.

Scholiasts coming from various disciplines have had their say as to the various origins and courses of Sarasvatī basing their arguments on various evidence ranging from Sanskrit literature to LANDSAT imagery and other modest techniques of research.

In fact, the Sarasvatī is the very soul of Indian culture. It is embedded in the entire fabric of Indian psyche. Since its inception, Sarasvatī and Indian culture both are interwoven. The origin of this great perennial culture of the world as Vedic culture owes its origin to the very origin of Sarasvatī. This culture flourished along the courses and tracks of Sarasvatī. More remarkably a loss of Sarasvatī is often counted, as is obvious from the statement of *Purāṇas*, towards the loss of ethical values of Indian culture. It is often discussed therein that due to the enormity of sin on the earth in Kaliyuga Sarasvatī went underground. Now we have started re-investigating the lost Sarasvatī. The more and more probes are being carried out, the more and more are we becoming conscious of our lost heritage, culture and ethos. The revival of Sarasvatī will certainly lead to the revival of the lost culture of Bhārata, the Vedic culture or say ancient most culture of the world.

Re-investigation of Sarasvatī is to reconstitute the

shattered fabric of Indian culture. This culture is, in fact, not constituted of philosophical and ethical values only but its physical structure is constituted among others, (viz. Himalayas, Mānasarovar, Gaṅgā etc.) of Sarasvatī. Sarasvatī represents one of the physical features of this culture. The actual revival of this culture lies in the revival of Sarasvatī. This culture had a strong fortress surrounded and safeguarded by the waters of Sarasvatī. With the drying up of its waters this culture was invaded by alien elements and so began to fizzle out. Hence now it has become imperative on our part to conduct a search for the lost course of Sarasvatī in order to give a new lease of life to the dying culture of this continent. This work has already been started at a large scale by number of scholars involving themselves at their own or in-groups. Most of their studies are based either on the interpretation of LANDSAT imagery or field verifications in the Indian part of the desert or archaeological remains associated with older river courses. Many scholars have though taken literary sources into account, but they are confined to describing the greatness and various epithets of mighty Sarasvatī. At the most, they have visualized its origin from the Himalayan mountains while recounting the literary sources. However, there is enormous and varied information lying scattered in the vast Vedic and post Vedic literature on Sarasvatī. The vast and extensive information providing data on various phases of existence of Sarasvatī has mixed up in a manner that it becomes very difficult for a lay scholar, who is not well conversant with the Vedic life and thought, to systematically classify and consolidate the scattered data phase-wise and thereby to present an integrated account of origin and changes in the flows of the river during various phases ranging from its origin to the age of *Mahābhārata* (5139 years ago) and afterwards. Though a number of terms attributing various aspects of Sarasvatī have appeared in the old Indian literature, but for want of proper orientation into the Vedic and Puranic dicta, nobody has so far been able to define and describe those terms in a manner that a proper picture of Sarasvatī through different ages may be presented and hence the scholars had to content themselves with the remarks that none of the ancient literatures systematically described the course of this river from its source to terminus. In view of the above assumptions, evidences from many sources including that of archaeological remains associated with old river courses, LANDSAT imagery and field verifications were gathered by the scholars to postulate their various theories as to the origin and flow of the river. The evidences from the archaeological remains associated with old river courses have suggested that a major river stemming from the same source as the present Sutlej, flowed through northern Rajsthan, Bahawalpur and Sind to the south east of the present course of the Sutlej and Indus in the third to second millennium BC (Allchin Goudie and Hegde, 1987). It is also suggested that the river used to flow through Raini and Wahind rivers and then through eastern Nārā and Hākrā in the Sind province of Pakistan to the Rann of Kutch (Oldham, 1893; Wadia 1938; Ali; Stein 1942; Krishan 1960; Wilhelmy 1969). The evidence gathered from the interpretation of aerial photography and LANDSAT imagery tend to prove that the Sarasvatī used formerly to flow through a more easterly course in the Rajsthan part of the desert when the luni river was one of its tributaries. Subsequently, the river shifted its course to the west several times and finally cut its contact with the Luni. (Ghose et al, 1978). The evidences from the aforementioned sources further lead to prove that when the river severed its link from Luni and shifted westward it did not occupy the Raini-Wahind-Nara–Hakra course in Pakistan (as suggested from archaeological evidences and earlier evidences from LANDSAT imagery but began to flow through another channel running through the present extreme desert terrain of Jaisalmer district in India and the Raini wahind–Nara–Hakra course is proved to be occupied by Sarasvatī later.

In course of such desperate modern attempts to ascertain the origin and route of sarsvatī the huge amount of information flooding the ancient Indian literature was totally neglected due only to the reason that all the terms related to

Sarasvatī river could not be defined and their historicity could not be established and the names of the places mentioned along the courses of Sarasvatī could not sequentially be located. Keeping in view the above fact, the whole exercise based on literary sources was taken to be futile and so was given a goodbye. On the other hand, the author of present lines finds that information on Sarasvatī is wide-ranging. The Vedas on the one hand, supply a good deal of data as to the spiritual, astronomical and geological origin of Sarasvatī and defines its relationship with other rivers as sisterly or motherly. The *Purāṇas* and Epics on the other hand shed an ample good light on the origin of Sarasvatī as well as its flow at different junctures by making a mention of the names of various places and *tīrthas* falling alongside the route of Sarasvatī. The need is to collect the whole data and to classify and consolidate the same rationally in view of various aspects of Sarasvatī and its existence at different stages and to analyze the same by co-relating it to the presently known factors. Keeping in view the desideratum of this type of an academic work on Sarasvatī based on ancient Indian literary sources, the present author makes an humble attempt to accomplish this uphill task briefly touching all the possible aspects.

1.1. Sarasvatī as mentioned in the Vedas

The word Sarasvatī finds its mention number of times in the Vedic literature including the *Saṁhitās*. The Vedic dicta is framed in a manner that each term has its equivalence in *adhyātma*, *adhidaivata* and *adhibhūta*. This fact has been pointed out by the present author from time to time. In the like manner Sarasvatī also has its equivalence in *adhyātma*, *adhidaivata* and *adhibhūta*. In ādhyātmika (spiritual) sense Sarasvatī signifies streams of knowledge, speech and mental faculties etc. In *adhidaivika* or astronomical sense, Sarasvatī represents cosmic aspects like rays of the sun as well as rainy waters. In adhibhautika or terrestrial sense Sarasvatī denotes terrestrial water flowing on the earth in the form of river.

The ancient Indian Vedic Scholiast Yāska interprets Sarasvatī as a river in physical sense. according to him

> *vāk nāmānyuttarāṇi saptapañcāśat. vāk kasmāt vacatetart sarasvatītyetarya nadi vaddevatavacca nigamā bhavanti.*
>
> (*Nigh. Naighaṇṭuka Kāṇḍa.* 7)

There are fifty-seven names of *Vāk devatā* or deity of speech. Speech is so called as it is spoken. In addition to the name *vāk*. Sarasvatī has been treated in the Mantras as river also.'

Hence it is established from the foregoing discussion that Sarasvatī in a physical and astronomical sense refers to *Nadī* in the Vedic dicta. It may, however, be pointed out here that most of the Classical Sanskrit terms which are often used in one conventional meaning or other do not hold the same conventional meaning as in the Vedas, for instance, the term *parvat* stands for mountains in Classical Sanskrit literature, but the same meaning does not hold good so far as the Vedas are concerned. In the Vedas *parvat* and all its synonyms refer to the cloud instead of a mountain. The ancient Vedic scholar Yāska has revealed this fact in his famous lexicon called Nighaṇṭu (1.10).

Several modern occidental, as well as oriental scholars, have held the observations of this great Vedic scholar as unfeasible. In fact, these scholars are not familiar with the Vedic culture. They consider this culture only 3-4 or at the most 10 thousand years old. They forget that this great perennial culture of the world is able to maintain its chronology since the time of its inception on the Earth i.e., from 197 crore years. In the light of the above facts, such observations of Yāska and many others seem to be unworkable and unfeasible in the present contest. The most of the modern scholars have preserved the ancient most remnants of this perennial cultural flow that emphatically suggests us that this culture is older than the Himalayas or say older than any mountain peak emerged on the globe. Since there originated no mountain on the earth in the beginning, hence the term parvat or its synonyms like adri, grāvā, giri, etc. were nothing to do with mountains, but rather used for clouds. Yāska observed in this connection as follows:

giriṣṭhā giristhāyī giriḥ parvataḥ samudgirṇo bhavati parvavān parvataḥ parva punaḥ pṛṇāteḥ pṛnātervardhamāsa parvadevasmin pṛṇantīti tat prakṛtitarat sandhi sāmanyāt meghasthya megho'pi giriretasmādeva

(*Nirukta*, 1.20)

'*Giri* is known as *parvat*, since it has been protruding above the surface of the earth. *Parvata* is so called, as it is constituted of fragments. It is so called as it brings up the living beings on the earth with water etc. These qualities are discernible in the cloud, hence a cloud is called g*iri*.'

Later these qualities were also associated with the mountains that emerged on the earth and hence the term *parvat* and its synonyms were also used later on for the mountains and de grado in grado this term got conventionalized for mountains only. This is why lord Macaulay laughs at the mention of *parvatas* flying in the sky. Had the poor Macauley been well conversant with the Vedic dicta, he would not have laughed, but would rather have enjoyed the Vedic wisdom. This example though is uncalled for here has been cited by the present author in order to re-orient the scholiasts into the Vedic life and thought. The author has taken up this subject separately in his work of book-length entitled *'Geological code of the Vedas.'*

A similar thing holds good for the term *Nadī* in the Vedas. The term *Nadī* in the Vedic period was used for celestial waters or say rainy waters only. This can very well be understood in the light of the following observations of the *Ātharvaṇa* seer. According to him, '*Nadī* is the name of water vapours contained in the clouds which produce the *Nadan* (thundering) sound on being discharged. This celestial river (*Nadī*) transforms into terrestrial one (*sindhu*) after falling from heaven (midsphere) in the form of raindrops.

(Arya:1995, 25)

In fact, this observation reveals such an early conditions

as the earth was devoid of any river system. Only the rainy waters used to irrigate it in the beginning. It was the rainy waters only that caused the flow of rivers on the earth in the beginning. This has clearly been observed by one of the Ṛgvedic seers as under:

sodañca sindhumriṇāt mahitvā vajreṇāna uṣasaḥ sampipeṣa ajavaso javinībhirvivṛścantsomasya tā mada indraścak (2.15.6)

To sum up, (*sindhu*) river was made to flow on the earth northward by *Indra* or charged cloud.

At another place seven rivers have been made to flow by *Indra* after killing the *Vṛtra* i.e. discharging a cloud:

yo hatvāhimariṇātsapta sindhun yo gā udajapāghā valasya yo aśmadotrantaragniṁ jajāna samvṛkṣamastsu sa janāsaindraḥ (2.12.3)

Thus it is obvious from the foregoing discussion that *Nadī* was used for rainy waters and the term *sindhu* was used for the waters flowing on the earth. Later on, when the flow of rivers and rivulets came into being on the earth, the same term (*Nadī*) was also applied to terrestrial rivers and hence it became the synonym for *sindhu*:

syandanā'imāḥ bhavanti sindhu nadanāḥ imā bhavanti śabdavatya. (Arya : 1995,26)

"Since the waters in the rivers flow, so they are called as Sindhu (having waters flowing in them). Since the waters flowing in the rivers produce sound, so the rivers are addressed as producing sound."

2

Sarasvatī as a Nadī

Thus it is clear from the foregoing discussion that Sarasvatī used to be a *Nadī* in the Vedic period so far as terrestrial and astronomical imports are concerned. In the astronomical sense it was the celestial river or precipitation in the form of rainy waters or snowflakes, originating from the clouds and in a physical sense, it was the terrestrial river that stored the rainy waters. As celestial river, it flowed northward, as has already been revealed in the observations of a Ṛgvedic seer (2.15. 6) that made the celestial river flow towards the north. Thus some northern point became the storehouse of the precipitation from clouds. This northern point was nothing else but a small crater on the surface of the earth popularly known as Mānas lake or Tethys sea as mentioned after the name of a modern geologist. Sarasvatī was the first terrestrial river carrying rainy waters to the Mānas-sara or Mānas crater or Tethys sea. Its name Sarasvatī also indicate the above phenomenon when etymologized in the words of Yāska, a great embodiment of Vedic life and thought. As per etymology, Sarasvatī consists of *saraṇa* i.e. flow of water towards the north. In fact, the first flow of water took place on the earth towards the north, hence the waters are called (*udaka*) only. (*Sarasvatī sara ityudakanām sartestadvatī)* and this *saraṇa* or flow of waters must have terminated into the Mānas-crater, so the Mānas-crater was called Mānas-sara.

3

Origin of Sarasvatī

The origin of Sarasvatī, as the Vedas had it, dates back to the very origin of waters on the earth. Apart from the Vedas, we do have Purāṇic and epic sources which record the age-old historical fact in connection with the origin of Sarasvatī. Since the period of the first origin of waters on the earth, three most significant geological events have taken place around the globe. First of all, it was the occurrence of the first glaciation in this region, which is said to have taken place 25 crore years ago. Secondly, it was the origin of Himalayan ranges of mountains seven crores of years back, as per modern geologists, or 12 crore years back as per Indian tradition. Thirdly the formation of Siwalik hills that took place way back from 20 lakh to 1 crore years ago. Given the above facts, we find the existence of the Sarasvatī into four phases. The first phase is pre-glacial period. Second is glacial, third is Himalayan and fourth is Post-Himalayan or Siwalik phase. Since the Vedic culture is Pre-Himalayan culture, as is obvious from the foregoing discussion, until and unless we take into account all the four phases, Vedic and such Purāṇic references dealing with the geological scenario of various phases appear only as contradictory and confusing and cannot be understood properly.

3.1 Sarasvatī in Pre-glacial phase

As per evidence gathered from Vedas and allegorical descriptions of the *Purāṇas* the origin of first Sarasvatī may be assigned to pre-glacial phase. According to the description of the Vedas, Sarasvatī owes its origin to clouds. The Ṛgvedic seer Vasiṣṭha has clearly indicated in his observations that Sarasvatī originates from the celestial p*arvatas.*

> *āno divo ghṛataḥ parvatad sarasvatī yajata gantu yajñam havaṁ devi jujusānā ghṛtāci sagmo vācamuṣati sṛṇotu*

> 'From the great celestial *parvata* (cloud) Sarasvatī flows towards the *yañīya* site. It hears the voice of a person who offers the oblation of *ghṛta* with the desire to receive it.'

The above mantra recalls the phenomenon of rainmaking.

Parvata, here, as discussed before, refers to a cloud and not a mountain what it means at present. Moreover, the use of word *divaḥ* 'celestial' pertains to the sky, which clearly supports the view that *parvata* was not taken for mountains in the Vedic age. Since there can be no other celestial *parvata* but the mountain, thus only clouds were referred to as such.

This was not only the observation of Vasiṣṭha, but the another seer had it the same way. According to him:

> *ekācetat sarasvatī nadīnām śuciryatī giribhya ā samudrāt.*
>
> (7.95.2)

> 'Sarasvatī the sacred among the rivers flows from the clouds to the sea.'

The above Vedic phrase has been interpreted by most of the scholars as 'from mountains to sea' in the conventional sense. It may thus suit their arguments that Sarasvatī flowed from the Himalayas to sea. In this way, all these scholars are able to read their pre-conceived notions regarding the origin of Sarasvatī. The fact is that the origin of none of the rivers was observed by seers from mountains as it is true today but from clouds. We have already discussed this issue in detail. The context will be summed up after quoting one more example to this effect. According to the Ṛgvedic seer of 1.14.5:

> 'Positive (*Agni*) and negative (*Soma*) charges in a cloud liberate water thereof by discharging *Vṛtra* or cloud.'

> *yuvaṁ sindhūnabhi sasteravadyādagnīsomā*

vamuñcataṁ gṛbhītān.

The above instance gives a candid support to the view that the Vedic seers saw rivers originating from clouds rather than mountains. Here it may also be maintained that in the first stage of the pre-glacial era, the flow of rivers was towards the north of the Mānas-sara. From the above-quoted statements of the Vedas, the origin of the second Sarasvatī from Mānas-sara or Tethys sea can also be understood easily.

3.2 Second stage of pre-glacial phase

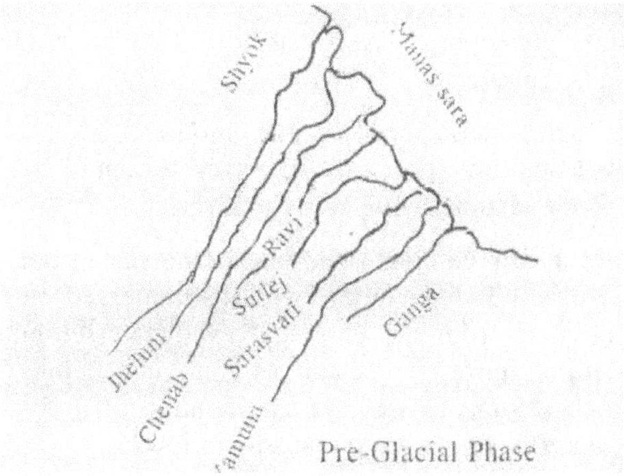

The second stage of the pre-glacial era was conspicuous with the overflowing Mānas-sara and the seven channels to drain its overflow. The overflow of Mānas lake was drained back down north by Sarasvatī and its six channels. This fact has also been disclosed by following observations of the Ṛgvedic seer.

varuṇa yasya te saptasindhavaḥ
anukṣaranti kākudaṁ sūrmyaṁ suṣiramiva

(*RV.* 8.69.12)

'O *Varuṇa*! (terrestrial storehouse of waters, i.e. Mānas-sara) seven channels of water issue from you and flow down to the lower parts like those of good veins'

Among seven channels specifically referred to above, Sarasvatī channel was known as the main channel, hence described by one of the seers as the seventh and mother of the six other channels.

ā yat sākaṁ yaśaso vāvaśānāḥ
sarasvatī saptathī sindhumātā
ya suṣvayanta sudughāḥ sudhārā
abhi svana payasā pinvamānāḥ (7.36.6)

taveme saptasindhavaḥ praśiṣaṁ soma sisrate
tubhyaṁ dhāvanti dhenavaḥ.

'There are seven channels that flow. They are running for you O! Soma .'

By being described as the mother, it is clear that Sarasvatī was the oldest and first river system of *Mānas Sara.* Rests of the channels followed Sarasvatī.

Here it may be mentioned that in the earlier period of the *RV.* Sarasvatī and six other rivers had emerged on the scene as is obvious from the earliest Ṛgvedic verse, but in later stages, three more river channels came into being. Since the latest period of *RV.* we find the mention of 9 rivers in one single *mantra*. The *mantra* reads as follows:

imam me gaṅge yamune sarasvatī
sutudri stomaṁ sacatāparuṣṇyā
asikniyā marudvṛdhe vitastāyā 'arjīkīyā
sṛṇuhyā suṣomayā (*RV.*10.75.5)

The above-cited *mantra* revealed to Vasiṣṭha has the mention of following eight rivers.

1. Gaṅgā 2. Yamunā 3. Sarasvatī 4. Śutudri 5. Paruṣṇi or Irāvati or Rāvi 6. Asikni or Chenab 7. Vitastā or Vyās 8. Suṣomā or Sohan.

Here it may be clarified that Sindhu has not been mentioned in the above *mantra* of *Nadī Sūkta* of *RV.* Several scholars have taken Suṣomā for Sohan river flowing in Atak situated in Pakistan. Yāska takes Suṣomā, keeping in view the absence of Sindhu, for Sindhu. This has also been made clear by Yāska in his *Nirukta* (9.25) while elaborating this *mantra*. He lays down as under:

> *suṣomā sindhuryadenāmabhiprasuvanti nadyaḥ.*
> *sindhu syandanāt*

'Suṣoma is Sindhu. Sindhu is so called as rivers submerged their basins into it. It is also so called as waters flow into it."

Thus from Yaska's interpretation, one thing is clear that by his time Suṣomā was present as the biggest river system allowing many rivers submerging into its basin. And Sarasvatī was no longer in existence since Yāska doesn't seem to have attributed such qualities to Sarasvatī.

Now a clear picture emerges that in the said mantra of *Nadī Sūkta* of *RV*. Sindhu doesn't find its mention. Here Suṣomā stands for Sindhu meaning a big river. In fact, in Yāska's *Nirukta* the term Sindhu doesn't signify the Sindhu river proper but a big river system. Maybe Suṣomā denoted Sohan flowing into Attock in Pakistan, as held by several other scholars. Under the circumstances, it may unhesitatingly be said that Sindhu was not in existence during the Ṛgvedic period. Here it may not be odd to mention that Sindhu and Brahmaputra have not been mentioned in any Saṁhitā of Veda. In the Veda, the mention of Sindhu has taken place as a common noun and not as a proper noun. In fact, the origin of Sindhu and Brahmaputra may to assigned to post Himalayan phase. This is why Vedic literature which was obviously composed before the origin of Himalayan ranges doesn't carry the mention of rivers originated quite late. In fact, Sindhu and Brahmaputra both find their origin from two separate parts of the same Mānas lake. This division into two streams took place only due to the upliftment of Himalayan ranges. Otherwise, both were virtually one and the same river system flowing downward instead of flowing towards west and east. This river system was known by then as Sarasvatī. It was flowing south-westwards.

Sarasvatī was the seventh river and is called as the

mother of six rivers. Presently this system is extant in the divided streams of Sindhu and Brahmaputra. Sindhu system still represents the same old six tributaries.

Thus it is clear that in the pre-glacial period Sarasvatī was a combined name of modern Sindhu and Brahmaputra and it had six tributaries and it flowed southwestward. The location of its course was between Yamunā and Sutlej. Since the *Nadī Sūkta* depicts it as third one starting from Gaṅgā as Gaṅgā-Yamunā-Sarasvatī-Sutlej-Ravi-Chenab-Jhelam-Vyāsa and Sohan. Origin of pre-glacial Sarasvatī may be assigned either to Clouds or to Tethys sea.

3.3 Glacial phase

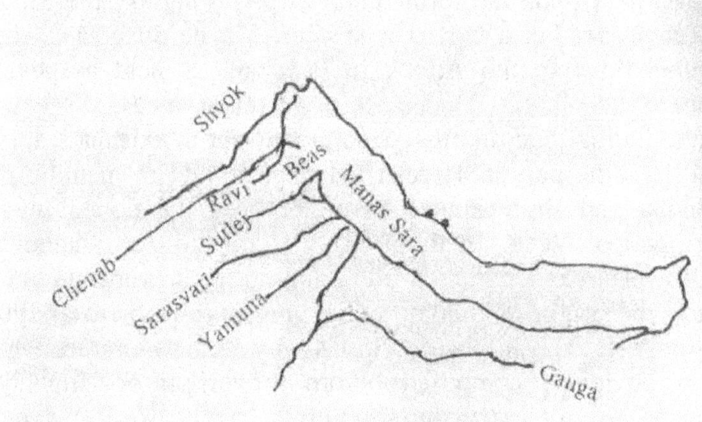

Glacial Phase

Glacial phase marks the period after the crust of the earth had emitted sufficient quantity of heat, the origin of waters had taken place on it in the form of Gaṅgā, Yamunā and Sarasvatī, etc. The first glaciation in this region of globe took place, as per modern geologists' calculations, in Triassic period, i.e. 22 crore years ago when the northern hemisphere consisting of the present-day Europe was still a desert and southern hemisphere consisting of Indian continent was covered with snow. The memory of this type of glaciation is alive in the records of extant traditions of *Purāṇas*. When the Tethys sea and its surrounding area witnessed the first ever glaciation, the origin of Sarasvatī changed from clouds or Mānas-sara to glaciers formed around Mānas-sara. There are clear cut indications in the Puranic traditions that Sarasvatī having approached the glaciers flowed through *Plakṣa*.

himvataṁ giriṁ prāpya plakṣāttatra vinirgatā

(*Skanda Pur*. 7. 30.41)

The approach of Sarasvatī to glaciers was its precipitation in the form of snowflakes from clouds and its flow in the form of waters on the earth has been assigned to a place known as *Plakṣa*. So, *Plakṣa* was the origin of the Sarasvatī during the glacial period and it was undoubtedly the period before the Himalayan ranges came into being.

Origin of Sarasvatī from *Plakṣa* has also been registered in the memories of traditions of other *Purāṇas* too, e.g. According to *Vāmana Purāṇa* (3-4), perennial Sarasvatī originated from *Plakṣa* tree.

plakṣavṛkṣāt samudbhūtā saricchreṣṭhā sanātanī (64.17)

In *Bṛhannāradīya Purāṇa* also Sarasvatī has been described as *Plakṣajātā* i.e. originated from *Plakṣa*.

mārkaṇḍeyena muninā saṁtaptaṁ paramaṁ tapaḥ
tatra tatra samāyātā plakṣajātā sarasvatī

In fact, *Plakṣa* during the glacial period marked the place where from the melted waters of glaciers flowed. That is why in the actual Vedic tradition of *Tāṇḍya Brāhmaṇa* (25.10.16) *Plakṣa Prasravaṇa* has been located as the actual place of origin of Sarasvatī. The term *Prasravaṇa* clearly indicates that *Plakṣa* was a place where from *srāva* or oozing of Sarasvatī took place. This oozing was nothing but the thawing of glacial ice at *Plakṣa*. Thus Sarasvatī's thawing out at *Plakṣa* was known as its origin from *Plakṣa* by then.

In *Tāṇḍya Brāhmaṇa* the distance between the place of vanishing (*Vinaśana*) and the point of rising of Sarasvatī has been measured as 44 *Āśvins.*

catuṣcatvāriṁsadaśvināni sarasvatyā vinaśanat plakṣaḥ prāsravaṇaḥ. *(25.10. 16)*

The distance between *Plakṣa* and *Vinaśana* is as long as 44 *Āśvin.*

4

Plakṣa

Now the main question arises as to what was the *Plakṣa*? Whether it was a name of a place or a tree, as has been remembered in several traditions. If it was a name of a place, how to locate it?

Plakṣa, in fact, was the name of a place, perhaps conspicuous with the presence of *Plakṣa* trees. Being replete with *Plakṣa* trees, it was called *Plakṣa*. So one should not get one self confused with *Plakṣa* as a tree or as a place. *Plakṣa* as a tree is often called in vernaculars as Pilakhana or fig tree known in botanical terms as *ficus religiosa*. Due to rising of Sarasvatī from a place surrounded by *Plakṣa* trees, *Plakṣa* assumed a religious fervor and the tree is considered to be holy. Such a place which was conspicuous with the presence of *Plakṣa* tree is today known as Pilakhua which is now located near Hapur or Garhgaṅgā in western UP. Pilakhua is obviously named after Pilakhana, a corrupt form of *Plakṣa*. Now the major problem is to establish the location of *Plakṣa* as modern Pilakhua as per literary records of Vedas, *Purāṇas* and Epics. In this regard a reference of *Vāmana Purāṇa* (3.4) that gives us an information of Post Himalayan scenario may be quoted. Accordingly, Sarasvatī after crossing thousands of hill-stones entered the Dvaitavana.

King Yudhiṣṭhir started from Kurujāṅgala towards the north on the banks of river Sarasvatī in search of some thick forest full of roots and fruits and after some time he entered Dvaitavana. There is also a reference of Paṇḍvas proceeding towards Sarasvatī located to the north of Marudhanvana (modern Meerut). Thus it is clear from the above cited references that route of Sarasvatī in glacial period was via

Deoband located to the north of Marudhanvana (Meerut). Next is the location of Kāmyakavana. According to chapter 244 of *Āraṇyakaparva,* Kāmyakavana was there almost in Marudeśa.' Here it may be clarified that Marudhanvana or Marudeśa was not meant by Marusthal or desert land but it signified Meerut only. From the north of Kāmyakavana began the forest of Himalayas. Thus the location of Dvaitavana (Deoband) on the banks of Sarasvatī and closeness of Dvaitavana and Kāmyakavana to Himalayan hills and forests respectively reveals that Sarasvatī flowed through UP and *Plakṣa* was nothing else but the modern Pilkhua. As per the author of the *Geography of Mahābhārata* (p. 213), from *Plakṣa Prasravaṇa*, Īsānudhyāsī tīrtha was at a distance of about half a mile. The name of the tīrtha is indicative of some place of worship, it can also be located in or around Pilakhua. So it can be established that modern Pilakhua in western UP was the *Plakṣa* of Post Saṁhitā glacial period. There is the possibility of glaciers extended up to Pilakhua. Due to glaciation, the region was called *Himvat* and there was the possibility of waters to have melted out of glaciers only up to the extent that they could have flowed till some place in modern Haryana boardering Rajasthan (*Vinaśana*). Location of *Plakṣa* as Pilakhua may also be understood on the basis of its reference in *Mahābhārata tīrtha Yātrā parva* (9.4) as

sarasvatī mahāpuṇyā hrādini tīrthamālini
yatra puṇyataraṁ tīrthaṁ plakṣāvatarṇaṁ śubham

Sarasvatī is a highly sacred river consisting of several ponds and *tīrthas* on its banks. The holy tīrtha named *Plakṣa* also lies on its banks. According to *Tāṇḍya Brāhmaṇa* (25.10.1-23) the distance from *Vinśana* to *Plakṣa Prasravaṇa* is 40 *Āśvins.* At the same distance from *Plakṣa* is situated *Svarga loka.* So the people who want to go to *Svarga loka* take a journey along with the stream of Sarasvatī.

catuścatvāriṁśdāśvināni sarasvatyā vinaśanvāt plakṣaḥ prāsravaṇaḥ tāvaditaḥ svargolokaḥ sarasvatīsammitena adhvanā svargaṁ lokaṁ yanti.

Here one thing must be known to the scholars that *Svarga loka* in the Sanskrit language Implies to the upper Himalayan ranges of mountains. Hence as per reference of *Tāṇḍya Brāhmaṇa* cited above, *Plakṣa* was situated at the equal distance from *Vinaśana* and Himalayan ranges of mountains. As has already been discussed, it was not situated on a hilly terrain rather this place was located in the plains down the mountain ranges. Under the circumstances, Pilakhua can only be the exact location for *Plakṣa*.

We came across a number of references in the *Brāhmaṇas*, which subscribe to the view that Himalayan ranges of mountains are *Svarga loka*.

According to *Jaiminīya Brāhmaṇa* (2.297-298) *Martyas*, desirous of winning the *Svarga loka* undertake the *ṣaḍrātra* sacrifice on the southern bank of Sarasvatī. They move against the stream to the *Devayāna* path or north direction. Against the stream or northward lies the *Svarga loka* and so they reach the *Svarga loka*.

athaite ṣadrātrāḥ. maruto vā akāmyantaujiṣṭhā bliṣṭhā bhūiṣ ṭhā viryavataṁ devānām syām jayema svargalokam iti. ta etaṁ ṣaḍrātraṁ yajñam apasyan - tenayajanta. Tesām sarasvatyā upamajjane dikṣā. dakṣiṇe tire dikṣante. sarasvatyā yanti. vāg vai sarasvatī. vāg u devayānaḥ panthāḥ. devayānenaiva tatpathā yanti. pratīpaṁ yanti. pratīpam iva vai svargo lokaḥ svarga eva tatlokaṁ pratipadyante.

In the same passage, it is stated that the sacrificer move to the east and north. *Svarga loka* is also located in the east. When they move eastward, they climb the *Svarga loka* only. (In fact, east-northerly direction has been specified for the *Svarga loka*). While moving east they go up to *Prakṣa Prasravaṇa* (afterwards they start moving northward). *Prasravaṇa* lies in the middle of *Devayāna mārga* or the path to *Svarga loka.* Where there is *Prakṣa Prasravaṇa*, there starts the *Svarga loka.* So from *Prakṣa Prasravaṇa* onward the sacrificer moves to *Svarga loka.*

prāñca udañca yanti. prāṅ iva ha vā idaṁ svargo lokaḥ svargaṁ eva tallokaṁ rohanto yanti, ā praksāt prasrvaṇād yanti. eṣa u ha vai vāco'nto yat prakṣaḥ prasravaṇaḥ. yatro ha vai vāco'ntas tat svargo lokaḥ svarga eva tallokaṁ gacchanti

At yet another place, *Jaiminīya Brāhmaṇa* (2.300) describes the place of origin of Yamunā (yamunotri) as the *Svarga loka*:

eva tallokaṁ gacchanti tāsāṁ yamunāvabhṛthaḥ eṣa vai svargo loko yad Yamunā Svargam.

It (3.150) also locates *Svarga loka* upstream the course of Yamunā. This also proves yamonotri as Svarga loka.

ukṣṇo vai randhraḥ kāvyo'kāmyatādbhiḥ pratīpaṁ svargaṁ lokam aroheyam sa ha sa yamunāyaiva pratīpam svargaṁ lokaṁ ārohat.

Thus it is clear from above cited references of *Jaiminīya Brāhmaṇa* that *Svarga loka* was nothing else but the hilly terrain of Himalayan ranges whence issued the Yamunā. So it is clear that the source of Yamunā was also situated 40 *Āśvins* from *Plakṣa* as that of the *Vinaśana. Pañcaviṁsa Brāhmaṇa* (25.10.21-23) clarifies that after reaching *Plakṣa Prasravaṇa*, the sacrificers had to climb up the mountainous terrain to reach the place named as kārapacava in order to have lustral bath into Yamunā.

yadā plakṣam prasravaṇam agcchntythotthānam kārapacavam prati yamunāvabhṛthamabhyavayanti

Āśvalayana Śrauta Sūtra (1917 : 443-6; 12,6) also prescribes *utthāna* ceremony after reaching Plakṣa Prasravaṇa and lustral bath at Kārapacava in Yumanā.

athotthānāni plakṣaṁ prasravaṇaṁ prāpyotthānam. Te yamunāyaṁ kārapacave'vabhṛthambhyuṣeyuḥ

Kātyāyana Śrauta Sūtra (1972 : 24.7-22) also prescribes the performance of Kāmyeṣṭhi at Plakṣa Prasravaṇa, whereas the lustral bath at Kārapacava in Yamunā. It is prohibited in Sarasvatī .

agnaye kamayeṣṭiḥ plakṣe prāsravaṇe. avabhṛthamabhyavayanti yamunāṁ kārapacavaṁ prati nāvabhṛtham sarasvatyām .

In the *Śalyaparva* of *Mahābhārata* (54.9-12) also Balarāma has been shown reaching Kārapavana after *Plakṣa*.

puṇyam tīrthavaraṁ dṛṣṭvā vismayaṁ paramaṁ gataḥ
prabhavaṁ ca sarasvatyāḥ plakṣa prasravaṇaṁ *balaḥ* (11)
samprāptaḥ kārapavanaṁ pravaraṁ tīrthm uttamam (12)

4.1 More on Plakṣa

The above hypothesis of *Plakṣa* being Pilakhua can be verified with the help of some more supportive evidences from *Mahābhārata.* After Yudhiṣṭhira, Kurujāṅgala and Sarasvatī region came under the domain of Parikṣita second. In fact, Kurujāṅgala and Sarasvatī regions were adjoining each other and *Plakṣa* was also situated in Kuru region. *Vanaparva* of *Mahābhārata* (83.84 chapters) also enumerates *Plakṣa* in the list of 113 *tīrthas* lying in Kuru region, *Plakṣa* is identified with modern regions of Thaneshwar, Delhi, Meerut and Bijnor between Sarasvatī and Gaṅgā rivers having its capital at Hastinapur near modern Bijnor (See also *Geographical Horizon of Mahābhārata* P.137) *Jain Ādi Purāṇa* (16.193) also locates Kurujāṅgala in between Sarasvatī and the river Gaṅgā.

According to some scholars, states lying from Pathankot-Jalandhar to river Yamunā and the southwestern forest near Kurukshetra (Thanesar) was also known as Kuru region.

Jāṅgala is also identified with the area around Bikaner, which was then known as Kāntārkaḥ. Thus from the foregoing discussion, it becomes explicitly clear that Kuru region or Kurujāṅgala was a vast area comprising of some states of modern Rajsthan, Punjab, complete Haryana and Meerut and Bijnor district of UP with its centre at Hastinapur.

Plakṣa was the terminal point of Balarāma's voyage.

Śalyaparva (54.10-11) of *Mahābhārata* Reads as follows:

sandhyā kāryāṇī sarvāṇinirvatyāruruhe'vcalam
nātiduraṁgatvā nagaṁ tāladhvajo balī
puṇyaṁ tīrthavaraṁ dṛṣṭvā vismayaṁ paramaṁ gataḥ
prabhavaṁ ca sarasvatyāḥ plakṣa prasravaṇaṁ balaḥ

This *Plakṣa* was obviously Pilakhua and not Ādibadri, etc. as mooted by several scholars. Most important point is that Gaṅgādvāra (modern Haridwar or Garh Gaṅgā is also enumerated as the area lying in Kuru region (*Mahābhārata Vanaparva*, Chapter 8.4.26).

The most striking thing is that in the list of various *tīrthas* enumerated in *Mahābhārata Vanaparva*, Gaṅgāsarasvatī Saṅgama has also been enumerated as one of the *tīrthas* (84.38) of Kuru region. This makes it very clear that the Sarasvatī and Gaṅgā must be crisscrossing each other at some place and this meeting place of Gaṅgā and Sarasvatī can be none other but Garhgaṅgā or Pilakhua. While recounting *Plakṣa* as the tīrtha of Kurukshetra, it is told that Sarasvatī originates from a Bamboo near Saungandhika vana (84.6-7). Location of Saugandhika vana has also been identified around river Mandākini of Garhwal hills of UP. At another place in *Mahābhārata* in *Vanaparva* (129.13) Yamunā tīrtha has been described as the holy *Plakṣāvataraṇa* and also as the doorstep of Himalayas (*nāka pṛṣtha*).

etadvai plakṣāvataraṇaṁ yamunā tīrthamuttamam
etadvai nākapṛṣṭhasya dvāramāhurmanīṣīṇaḥ

In the *Skand Purāṇa* (7.33.40-41), it has been described that Sarasvatī as a river emerges from a glacier and comes down to the earth at *Plakṣa*.

tato visṛjya tāṁ deviṁ nadī bhūtvāsarasvatī
hiṁvataṁ giriṁ prāpya plakṣātatra vinirgatā
avatīrṇā dharā pṛṣṭh. ..

The above facts make two things explicitly clear that earlier Sarasvatī found its origin from a glaciated region near Saugandhika Vana around Mandākini. Here it may not be odd to relate a folk tale of Bhutias of Mana village lying In the Garhwal region of Utter Pradesh. The folk tradition of the villagers remembers the origin of Sarasvatī in the region of Mānā pass at an altitude of 18,400 feet above sea level. The pass is surrounded by high peaks covered with a huge mass of snow and ice and lies on the old trade route along Indo-Tibetan border to Garhwal region of Uttar Pradesh. From Mānā pass to Mānā village, the Sarasvatī covers a distance of 45 kms. in the high altitude region of the Himalayas. The altitude varies from 11,000 ft. at Keshava Prayāg (the meeting point of Sarasvatī with Alaknandā) more than 18,000 ft. at the origin. As per the folk tale the river goes down to *Pātāla loka* from the Bhima bridge, leaving a small stream to meet Alaknandā. The rest of the river reappears at Prayāga Rāja to form the Triveṇī. The fact is that before its junction with Alaknandā at Keshav Prayāg, the Sarasvatī falls in a deep and narrow gorge below Bhima bridge reportedly made by one of the five famous Pāṇḍva brother Bhima, during the 12 years long wandering period of the Pāṇḍvas. The gorge is 100 to 200 feet deep. The river Sarasvatī emerges from the gorge after its sound and fury in white caps and meets Alaknandā to form Keshav Prayāg.

Thus from the local tradition of folk tales also it is crystal clear that *Plakṣa* was a place below glaciated region and during *Brāhmaṇika* period most probably it was Pilakhua. Later due to the origin of Himalayas when Sarasvatī lost its very existence, its origin was sought into the origin of Yamunā.

Here it may specifically be mentioned that during the period of *Mahābhārata, Sarasvatī* (southern stream of Yamunā) was no longer a flowing river. It was in the process of drying up. Balrāma's voyage of Sarasvatī from its terminus to source only refers to the memory of various places and *tīrthas* handed down to him through a tradition of thousands of years. Balarāma didn't travel along the live track of Sarasvatī, rather he only visited the various famous places known by his time to have located once along the banks of the Sarasvatī. During the course of thousands of years, Sarasvatī changed many flows. Therefore it would be a great folly to locate all the places traversed by Balarāma along one single track.

5

Vinaśana

After determining the location of Plakṣa, we may now come to *Vinaśana*. *Vinaśana* has been recognised as the point of terminus of Sarasvatī. During post Saṁhitā period or glacial period, Sarasvatī never terminated in the western sea. It was only during the Himalayan phase that Sarasvatī started terminating into the sea. So during this phase, instead of western sea, it flowed till *Vinaśana* and lost there itself in the dry desert. *Vinaśana* has so far been a disputed and hotly debated issue. Some historians and archaeologists locate it near Bharner, others near Kālibaṅgā and some others place it in Rajasthan. However, they ignore the popular convention of the *Purāṇas* that *Vinaśana* falls in the Kurukshetra region. The reason why Kurukshetra was called *Vinaśana* has been cited by Trikāṇḍaśeṣa as under:

vinaśana (vinasyati antardadhati sarasvatyatreti)
kurukshetra. tacca hastināyā uttarpascime vartate.

'*Vinaśana* (where Sarasvatī went underground) is in the Kurukshetra region and lies to the north west of Hastinapur.'

Vinaśana has also been enumerated in the list of *tīrthas* lying in the Kurukshetra region.

Under the circumstances, *Vinaśana* can be a place close to Kurukshetra or fall in the boundary of Kurukshetra region. *Padma Purāṇa* (18.247) locates the site of *Vinaśana* as far down stream as Puṣkarāraṇya .

puṣkarārṇyamāsādya punastasmāt sarasvatī antardhānaṁ gatā gantuṁ pravṛttā paścimābhimukhi

The above reference of *Skanda Purāṇa* (Nirṇayasāgar Press, *Nāga*ra *Khaṇḍa*, 164.39) appears to state that the flow of the river Sarasvatī went underground after it reached Puṣ karāraṇya in her tendency to move towards west.

In fact, Puṣkarāraṇya of Kurukshetra was the forest area located close to present Jind or Jayantikā. Still, this place is famous as Pokharan. There is a pond, which is known even today as a pond where did Duryodhana hide himself after being defeated by Bhima in mace fighting. So it is crystal clear from this reference that Vinaśana is located in Haryana itself and not in Rajasthan. The area of Bisan in Rohtak is situated downward the Puṣkarāraṇya. Moreover, Beri or ancient Badri Aśram is close to Bisan and still famous as a holy place and is replete with numerous temples.

Sridharasvāmī (c1400 AD) cited by C. Rayachaudhuri (1958 :134), in his gloss on *Bhāgavata Purāṇa* (1.9.1) locates *Vinaśana* in Kurukshetra itself. The fact is that during the age of composition of *Brāhmaṇas* and *Sūtras*, when the sacrificial cult was at its climax, the name of *Vinaśana* stuck to one particular locality, which almost constantly remained humming with all sorts of sacrificial activity. As we have already described Beri close to Bisan being such a holy place, the geographical identification of *Vinaśana* of Kurukshetra region with the area of Bisan near Beri of Rohtak will not be farfetched one.

One more striking feature that subscribes to the very hypothesis of the present author is that *Vinaśana* has been described in Bhāgavata (1.9.1) a place in the vicinity of Kurukshetra where did Bhiṣma fall after the end of his 18 days' fighting.

iti bhitaḥ prajā drohātsarvadharma vivitsayā
tato vanaśanaṁ prāgāt yatra devavrato'patat

Bhāgavata Purāṇa (10.79.23) has again mentioned *Vinaśana* as a place where did Balarāma go to forestall the mace-duel between Bhima and Duryodhana.

sa bhima duryodhanayor gadābhyāṁ yudhyatormṛdhe
vārayiṣyan Vinaśanaṁ jagāma yadunandanaḥ

In fact, mace-duel, as stated above, took place in the vicinity of Kurukshetra. The modern Bisan in Rohtak is a place close to Pokharan in Jind where did Duryodhana on having been defeated in mace duel hide himself. *Bhāgvata* has described it as a place of Bhisma's fall as well as a place of mace-duel between Bhima and Duryodhana. In fact, the mace-duel between Bhima and Duryodhana took place at a site close to the site of Bhisma' falls. Moreover, Pokharan pond, where did Duryodhana hide himself, is also not very far. So the author won't be erring in any way if he identifies *Vinaśana* with modern Bisan close to Beri in Rohtak.

So it may be established that modern Bisan was the place of Sarasvatī's disappearance in Brāhmaṇic period.

etad vinaśanam nāma sarasvatyā viśāmpate
dvāraṁ niṣādarāṣṭrasya yeṣām dveṣāt sarasvatī
praviṣṭā pṛthiviṁ vīra mā niṣādā hi māṁ viduḥ

(*Mahābhārata Vanaparva*, 130.3-4)

The *Baudhāyana Dharmasūtra* (1.2.10) describes Āryavartta as the country lying to the east of Adarśana (which may probably be the *Vinaśana*), west of Kālakavana, south of the Himalayas and north of Pariyātra.

prāgdarśanātpratyakkālakavanādakṣiṇena himavantamudak pariyātram etadāryavarttam.

Vasiṣtha Dharmasūtra (Kane, 1941: vol.ii, P.13) repeats the same description verbatim with the substitution of Adarśa by Adarśana. So does *Mahābhāsya* of Patañjali (2.4.10). In *Manusmṛti* (2.21) Kālakavana is replaced with Prayāga while giving the same geographical description to Madhyadeśa which is equated with Āryavartta. This is repeated in the *Abhidhānacintāmaṇi* of Hemacandra (3.17) and *Kāvyamimāṁsā* of Rājaśekhara (Ch.2) who also describes another central region, which he calls *Antarvedī*, as lying between *Vinaśana*, Prayāg, Gaṅgā and Yamunā.

vinaśanaprayagayor gaṅgā yamunāyoścantarmantar veda

(Ch.17)

Puruṣottamdeva, the author of *Trikāṇḍaśeṣa*, describes *Vinaśana* as Kurukshetra:

kurukśetraṁ vinaśanaṁ kauśāmbi vatsapaṭṭanam

(2.1.14)

Śabdakalpadruma places it in northwest of Hastinapur

tacca hastināyā uttarapaścime vartate .

In *Mahābhārata* (9.36.2), we also find a reference that narrates that the loss of Sarasvatī adversely affected the Abhiras and Śudras inhabiting along the banks of Sarasvatī during that period. *Mahābhārata* (*Śalyaparva*, 36.1 and *Vanaparva* 130.3-4) allegorically relates this fact as if Sarasvatī was envious with Śudras and Abhiras.

śudrānabhīrān prātidveṣād yatra naṣṭā sarasvatī
yasmāt sā bharataśreṣṭha dveṣānnaṣṭā sarasvatī
tasmāttad ṛṣaya nityaṁ prāhurvinaśaneti ca

Now to locate the actual point of disappearance of Sarasvatī, we shall have to locate the settlements of Abhiras and Śudras. Śudras and Abhiras usually settled over the banks of Sarasvatī during *Mahābhārata* period. It was this class of people that mostly suffered due to the disappearance of Sarasvatī. Location of settlements of the above-mentioned castes in the area of Rajasthan, Gujrat and Haryana may be of significant help to locate the lost track of Sarasvatī in this region. In fact, the region of Haryana is said to have been populated immensely by Abhiras in ancient times. This is why one of the reasons of nomenclature of Haryana is also assigned to the term Abhirāyana-Abhirāyaṇa-Ahirāyaṇa-Haryana.

On the basis of foregoing discussion, it can be maintained that *Vinaśana* was some place in Kurukshetra region. Here it may also be made clear that Kurukshetra was not a particular place like the present one, rather it was a vast area lying between the Gaṅga and Sarasvatī. As such *Vinaśana* may be located as Bisan of Rohtak, as this place is close to Bṛhadāraṇyaka.

Hemachandra's and Rajasekhara's description of *antervedī* between *Vinaśana* and Prayāga, Yamunā and Gaṅgā supports the location of *Vinaśana* close to the basin of Yamunā and the area represented by Bisan in Rohtak being such a place. Thus the Bisan hypothesis of *Vinaśana* is strengthened by all means.

Apart from this, it would be justified to say that for want of some strong evidence, scholars have tried to twist the literary proof to suit their preconceived notions and conjectures.

To quote the views of a few scholars, OP Bharadvaja describes it as Kalibangan. Oldham (*J.R.A.S.* 1893, series-3, vol. 25.P.52) places it near Sirsa. N.L. Dey (1971 : 131), B.C. Lal (P.16); and D.C. Sircar (1971 : 47) agree with Oldham in locating it near Sirsa. Rahul Sankrtyayana (1957 : 8) locates it not far from the confluence of the Chenab and Sutlej and also even close to the Indus.

Gazetteer of Ambala District (P.7) identifies it with Bhatner, which is the same as Hanumangarh. N.N. Godbole (1963: Intro.P.1) Krishan (quoted by Godbole, P.18) and Saxena (1976: 10) agree with the view of Ambala Gazetteer. S.K. Belvelkar (quoted by R.K. Dvivedi, 1975:173) describes *Vinaśana* as the desert in Ambala and Sirhind while Wadia (1976: 368) calls it the sands of Bikaner Dist. H.C. Rayachaudhury (1972: 368) puts it near the track in the lower Indus valley and western Rajputana, while M.L. Bhargava (1964: 83) recognises it somewhere above Sardargarh and Probably at or about Suratgarh. *The Vedic Āge* (ed. Majumdar R.C. 1957: 251) like *Vedic India* (third Reprint,1967, vol.ii, P.300) confines it to Patiala Dist. And Indhas (1967:145-1, P.92) finds it in the Khadal tract about the Derawar fort in Cholistan Tehsil in Bahawalpur Dist. of Pakistan.

All the above-cited views are conjectures, which are postulated on the basis of the visible current of modern Mārkaṇḍā and Ghaggar as Sarasvatī. The fact is that *Vinaśana* was quite famous till *Mahābhārata* period. Though the now memory of its location has faded away but it might not have lost its linguistic identification. So locating *Vinaśana* without linguistic similarity would be a futile exercise. From the above reference, it is crystal clear that the postulations of modern historians and archaeologists are false and quite misleading. In fact, this place falls in the boundaries of modern Haryana. Remnants of this place still exist in the name of a place called Bisan in Rohtak district of Haryana. So Bisan of Haryana may be known as the point of the terminus in the Vedic Sarasvatī. It is situated to the north-west of Hastinapur also. So one should not be misled by the conjecture of modern historians and archaeologists in the matter of *Vinaśana.*

With the identification of locations of Plakṣa and *Vinaśana* as Pilakhua and Bisan respectively, the problem of the distance between two points also gets solved. As per *Tāṇḍya Brāhmaṇa* the distance between Plakṣa and *Vinaśana* is 44 *Āśvins. Āśvin* is a unit of measurement equated to about 5 *krośas.* This distance comes about 220 *krośas*, which is amost the same as is between Bisan of Rohtak Haryana and Pilakhua, UP.

In fact, both of these places were known by the time of *Mahābhārata* War, so their location is not difficult to identify if due care is taken in locating them afresh.

During this period Sarasvatī used to flow towards west.

pratyaṁmukhi khalu Sarasvatī pravahati

(*Tāṇḍya Br.* 2.22.18)

6

Himalayan Phase

6.1 Early Himalayan phase

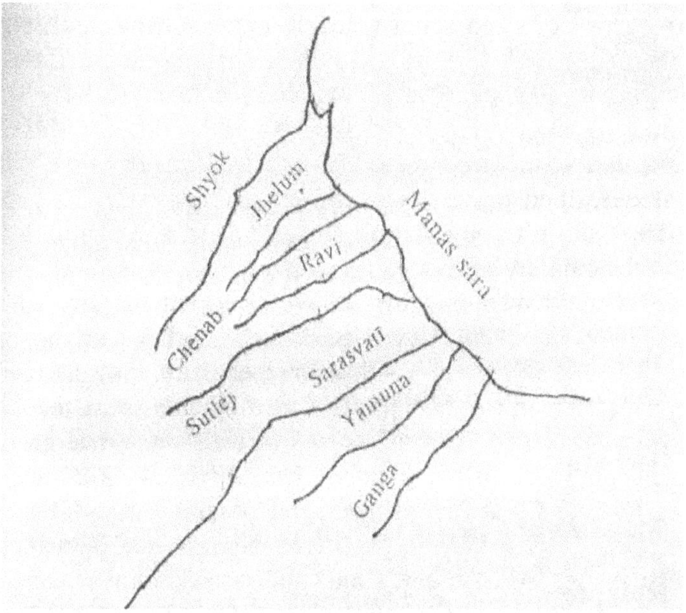

Early Himalayan Phase

6.1.1 Origin of Himalayan ranges of mountain

There are many cues registered in the *Purāṇas*, regarding the origin of Himalayan ranges of mountains. Before the origin of Himalayan ranges Sarasvatī used to emerge from the glaciated region of Tethys sea named as *Plakṣa* or present day Pilakhua. This fact has already been established by the present author. *Skanda Purāṇa* (*Prabhāsa khaṇḍa* 33.89) records an alarming event of geological history that while emerging from *Plakṣa* at the glaciated region (*Himvat* place), Sarasvatī flowed to the west, it was obstructed on its way by a mountain wanting to marry her forcibly. This record sheds an ample good light on the Sarasvatī's flow during the glacial period before the origin of Himalayas. It also tells allegorically that when the upper Himalayas began to form, it came in the way of Sarasvatī as if it wanted to marry her forcibly. The Puranic records further reveal that Sarasvatī pretended to take bath before the matrimonial ceremony and entrusted fire to the mountain which was immediately burnt down. This points to some volcanic upheaval that took place by that time. This is said to have happened in *Cākṣusa Manvantara* (*Skanda Purāṇa*, *Prabhāsa khaṇḍa* 35.34). Thus we may assign this happening to the end of *Cākṣusa Manvantara.* Since again in *Vaivasvata Manvantra* the same fire is described to have broken out as *Aurvānala.* This time the fire was quite devastating since it started consuming the earth immediately after its emergence (*Skanda Purāṇa* 35.6). However, Sarasvatī is said to have confined the fire to the ocean only i.e. Tethys sea. Sarasvatī is also said to have carried the *Aurvānala* in a golden pitcher and taking its rise at Pippalādāśram in the Himalayas it flowed westward reaching Kedāra where it pierced the earth's crust to go underground with burning fire in her hands (*Skanda Purāṇa* 33.21-26). It broke forth again at Bhuteshwar after passing through Srikaṇṭ ha deśa, Kuruksetra, Viraṭanagara, Gopāyangiri, Kharjuribana, Mārkaṇḍeyāśram and Arbudāraṇya (*Skanda Purāṇa* 35. 30-41). The above record of the *Purāṇa* also implies a slow process of formation of Himalayas through volcanoes at the end of *Cākṣuṣa Manvantara.* But the process gained momentum with the beginning of *Vaivasvata Manvantara.* At the end of *Cākuṣusa Manvantara* the volcanic Lava was treated as *Vaḍvānala*, but in the beginning of *Vaivasvata Manvantara* the same was treated as *Aurvānala.* First the Puranic record reveals that the formation of the first phase of Himalayan ranges commenced some where around 12 crores years ago at the end of *Cākṣusa Manvantara*. Contrary to this the modern scientists consider the origin of the Himalayas around 7 crores years ago. The modern view is based on estimates, whereas ancient view is based upon the actual happening observed and recorded by the then *Ṛṣis*. The above records point out that in the process of carrying *Vaḍvānala* i.e. lava erupted due to the formation of Himalayas, Sarasvatī vanished underground.

Skanda Purāṇa (35.14) also predicts the birth of another *Vaḍvānala* at the end of current *Manvantara* that implies a connection between *Vaḍvānala* (volcanic eruption at the submarine level) and a deluge that is traditionally associated with the end of *Manvantara* cycle.

Thus even if we go by modern geological researches, the Himalayan ranges of mountains began to form in the Eocene period i.e. around 7 crore years ago. It is the established fact that the Himalayan ranges of mountains formed from volcanoes. Submarine volcanic activities have been reported in the tradition of *Purāṇas* in the name of *Vaḍvāgni*. *Vaḍvāgni* is nothing else, but the submarine volcanic activity. Age old Puranic traditions (*Skanda Purāṇa* 7.33.40-41) holds that Sarasvatī drained *Vaḍvāgni* to western sea at Prabhāsa Pāṭan. This tradition

obviously points to the geological event that took place 12 crore years ago due to volcanic activity at the submarine level of Mānasa-sara or Tethys sea. The upliftment of the bottom took place due to continuous deposition of volcanic lava. This upliftment of the bottom caused the dewatering of Mānas-sara. The outflow of the uplifted Mānas-sara was drained by Sarasvatī towards the western sea at Prabhās Pāṭ an. In fact, only in the early Himalayan phase i.e. 12 crores years ago when Himalayan ranges were under the process of formation, Sarasvatī found its way towards the western sea or say it terminated at the sea. Thus it can be informed that since the inception of glacial period, i.e. 22 crore years ago till the beginning of the formation of Himalayan ranges, i.e.

12 crore years ago, Sarasvatī rose from *Plakṣa* and flowed till *Vinaśana*, but with the rise of Himalayan ranges Sarasvatī's course extended to the western sea. The extended route of Sarasvatī remained in operation till the formation of the last phase of Himalayan ranges came into being (i.e. from 12 crore years ago till about 2 crores years ago.). 2 crores years being the period when Lord Rama ruled this country. As per Indian chronology, Rama was born in the beginning of 24th *Tretā* which works out to be around 1.8 crore years.

Here it may again be summarised for the convenience of the readers that in the *Saṁhitā* period, which according to the present author lasted from 197 crores years till glacial period, i.e. 22 crore years ago, Sarasvatī is described to have originated from clouds to form water stores on the earth. In the post-*Saṁhitā* or *Brāhmaṇa* period, the period of presence of first ever glaciers in this region, as the present author calls it, Sarasvatī originated from *Plakṣa* and flowed till Vinśana or the area close to modern Bisan of Rohtak District of Haryana. It is the Puranic tradition dating as early as the origin of the Himalayas that remembers the Sarasvatī having drained the *Vaḍvānala* of Tethys sea to the western sea. Thus in the early Himalayan phase, Sarasvatī originated in the form of overflowing waters of Tethys sea.

6.2 Middle Himalayan phase

Middle Himalayan phase marks the period before the origin of Siwalik ranges i.e. 6 crore years ago. We meet with such references in the Purāṇas as register origin of Sarasvatī during this phase. According to the tradition of Matsya Purāṇa (121.64-65), Sarasvatī and Jyotiṣmatī rivers flowing towards western and eastern seas respectively issued from the Sarpa or Nāga lake situated at the back side of Hemakūṭa.

parasaparena dviguṇā dharmataḥ kāmato'rthataḥ
hemakuṭasya pṛṣṭhe tu sarpāṇām tatsaraḥ smṛtaḥ
sarasvatī prabhavati tasmātjjyotiṣmatī tu yā
avagāḍhe hyubhayataḥ samudrau purvapaścimau

(121. 65)

Vāyu Purāṇa (*Gaṅgā Avatāra varṇana*, Chap 47) depicts the same fact only with a few minor variations, e.g. *Sarpa* or *Nāga* lake has been mentioned as Śayanā lake and Sarasvatī has been mentioned as Manasvinī. In the reference given above, Hemakūṭa, modern Kailash range (Ali, 1973 : Chap. 4) and the *Sarpa* lake or Śyanā lake at the back of Kailāśa is the lake Nak Tso which with the Pangong Tso forms an extensive water sheet that joins the Shyok at its southeastern bend and then combined waters flow towards the western sea (Ali: 71)

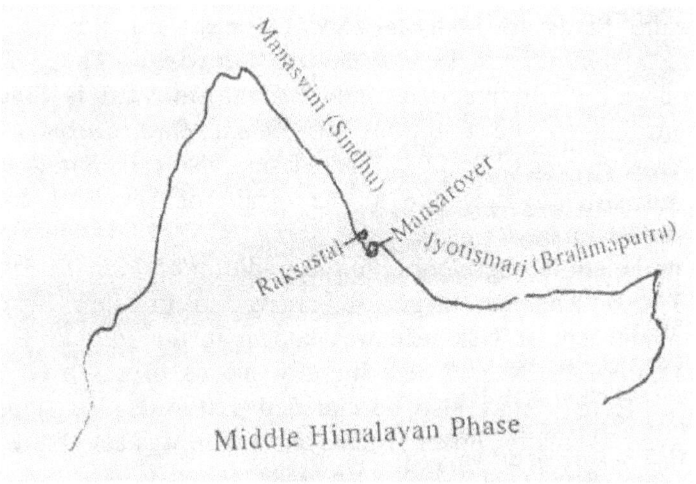

Vedic Sarasvatī divided into two streams Sindhu and Brahmaputra leading to its end

Ali seems to be correct in his inferences. The word Hemkūṭa signifies the Kailāśa. In fact, *Sarpa* lake or *Nāga* lake or Nak Tso has known in *Vāmana Purāṇa* as Brahma Sarovar also. Brahma-sara is indicative of Mānas-sara. Maybe in the more ancient time Nak Tso had extended upto the modern Manasarovar lakes (Mānasarovar and Rākṣ astāla). Today also we find two river systems Sindhu and Brahmaputra issuing from Mansarovar lakes, i.e. Sindhu from Mānasrovar and Brahmaputra from Rākṣasatala, whereby Sindhu enters into western sea and Brahmaputra into eastern sea. *Matsya Purāṇa* names Sindhu as Manasvinī due to its origin from Mānasrovara and while *Vāyu Purāṇa* names it as Sarasvatī only. On the other hand, Brahmaputra has been named as Jyotiṣmatī by both since it flows towards east or the direction of Prāga jyotiṣpur (Assam). Jyotiṣmatī is the name of eastern direction because the Sun rises first in the east. This is why, Assam was called Prāga jyotiṣpur. Thus Sarasvatī in middle Himalayan phase is Sindhu. In fact, both the rivers Sindhu and Brahmaputra issue from the two parts of the same lake. Perhaps, this is why the tradition of *Padma Purāṇa* (5.18;117-28; 123) and *Skanda Purāṇa* (7.35.26) recalls Sarasvatī both as *Prācī* or eastward flowing and *Paścimābhimukhi*, i.e. westward flowing. Thus *Prācī* Sarasvatī is Brahmaputra and *Paścimī* Sarasvatī is Sindhu, according to the traditions of *Padma Purāṇa* (ibid.) and *Skanda Purāṇa* (7.35.26). Trikāṇḍaśeṣa also calls Sarasvatī as Jyotiṣmatī. In fact, due to the origin of Sarasvatī during middle Himalayan phase from *Sarpa* or *Nāga* lake, its origin is assigned to *Nāgodbheda* in the tradition of *Vāmana Purāṇa* (13.120). Thus the origin of Sarasvatī from Manas lake or Brahma lake or Nak lake was known in the *Purāṇa*s as the *Nāgodbheda. Nāgodbheda* literally means origin from Nak lake. Here it may also be clarified that Nāk also signifies heaven. Actually, upper Himalayan region was also known as or famous as heaven or *Svarga loka.*

6.3 Last Himalayan Phase

In the last Himalayan phase, we find the origin of Siwalik hills. The whole Himalayan region in the earliest glacial period was famous as *Himvat* region. After the Himalayan ranges of mountains start originating the region came to be known as Kailash region or the abode of Śiva. Later on, the hilly terrain that developed at the lower region of Kailāśa came to be called as flocks of Śiva or Śivālaka or Śiwalik in the present sense of terms. With the origin of Siwalik ranges, the origin of various rivers also shifted from Upper Himalayan region (*Svarga loka* or *Nāga* ***loka***). Śivālaka ranges were also called as *Himvatpāda* being the last phase of the origin of Himalayan mountains. Take for instance the origin of Gaṅgā. Gaṅgā is also described in *Purāṇas* to have first originated from *Svarga loka*. *Svarga loka* is both the midsphere (atmosphere) where do the clouds form and precipitate into the form of rain or the highest altitudes on the earth,i.e. Upper Himalayan region and two polar regions (*Merus*), i.e. North pole and South pole. About the origin of Gaṅgā, it is stated that from *Svarga* it fell upon the flocks of the Śiva. Flocks of the Śiva, as stated earlier, are nothing else but the Siwalik ranges of mountains. From flocks of Śiva, Gaṅgā is stated to have come down on the earth in various streams. Similarly, during Siwalik phase, Sarasvatī's origin is also narrated to be *Śivodbheda*, i.e. the origin of Sarasvatī from Siwalik ranges of mountains. Siwalik ranges were also known as *Himavatpāda*, being the last phase of the origin of Himalayas. *Brahma Purāṇa* (2.16.24-27) furnishes a list of rivers originated during *Himavatpāda*, or Siwalik phase. The list reads the names Yamunā, Saryu, Rāvī, Vyāsa, Jhelam, Devikā, Kuhu, Gomati, Dṛṣadvatī, Kauśikī, Tridiva, Niṣṭhivī, Gaṇḍakī, Cakṣu and lohita as under:

tairvimiśrā janapadā āryā mlecchāśca bhāgasaḥ
pīyante yairimā nadyo Gaṅgā sindhuḥ sarasvatī -24
śatadruścandrabhāgā ca yamunā saryustathā

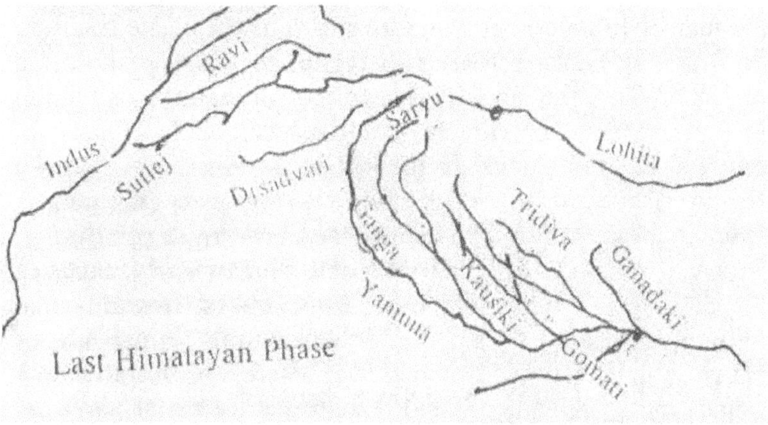

irāvatī vitastā ca vipāśā devikā kuhū - 25
gomatī dhūtapāpā ca budbudā ca dṛṣdvatī

kauśikī tridivā caiva niṣṭhivī gaṇḍakī tathā -26
cakṣurlohitā ityetā hiṁvatpādanissṛtāḥ -27

The tradition of *Brahma Purāṇa* referred to above, clearly reveals that in the last phase of origin of Himalayas Saryū, Devikā, Kuhu, Gomatī, Dṛṣadvatī, Kauśikī, Tridivā, Niṣṭ hivī, Gaṇḍakī, Cakṣu and Lohita figure either as new rivers or old rivers with new names. In the context of old rivers with new names, mention may be made of Lohita or present day Brahmaputra. It hadn't assumed its entity as Lohita in the earliest phase of the origin of Himalayas. In the earliest phase, it was named as Jyotiṣmatī as stated earlier. In fact, In pre Himalayan period Sindhu and Lohita were not in existence. Their combined name was Sarasvatī. It is during Himalayan period only that both the river systems came into being by dividing Sarasvatī into two oppositely flowing streams and it was the last phase of Himalayan origin that they assumed an entity separate from that of Sarasvatī. It is the last phase of Himalayan origin that we find a shift in the connection of Sarasvatī from Sindhu or Jyotiṣmatī to Gaṅgā. Its origin was also recalled as Śivodbheda like that of Gaṅgā's Śivālak. *Brahma Purāṇa*, the tradition of which deals with the information about Siwalik phase, also narrates a story to reflect an ample good light on a geological fact that Sarasvatī submerged itself into the basin of Gaṅgā owing to the fear of Brahma's growing love towards her. The tradition of *Brahmavaivarta Purāṇa* also relates to one and the same origin of Sarasvatī and Gaṅgā. In fact, after the completion of the last phase of Himalayan ranges the whole Himalayan region became famous as the region of Śiva. The eastern region also came to be known as region of Brahmā or Brhmarṣideśa which is represented by modern Burma. Sarasvatī's fear of growing love of Brahmā clearly indicates the drainage of maximum waters of Sarasvatī towards east through its eastern stream, i.e. Brahmaputra. To maintain its entity as the westward flowing river, there was no other way round, but to remain contended with the myth that Sarasvatī submerged itself into the basin of Gaṅgā. The same myth developed and it was stated, as shown in the tradition of

Brahmavaivarta Purāṇa, that Sarasvatī and Gaṅgā had same origins,

The one and sameness of Gaṅgā and Sarasvatī is also substantiated by a tradition of *Vāmana Purāṇa* (Chap. 42) where it is ruled that if one takes a dip into the eastern flow of Sarasvatī, he gets the benefit of taking a dip into Gaṅgā.

yaḥ snāti gaṅgā snānaphalaṁ labheta pūrvapravāhe

In fact, the mention of eastern flow in connection with Sarasvatī is a pointer to Gaṅgā only and nothing else.

The connection between Sarasvatī and Gaṅgā could also be established from the point that the Vedic origin of Sarasvatī was called from *Plakṣa*. Ancient *Plakṣa* or Pilakhua in modern times, as proved earlier, being situated at a point close to the basin of Gaṅgā. Close to the same point is a place called Garhgaṅgā or the home of Gaṅgā. In this way, the original source of Vedic Sarasvatī (*Plakṣa*) and Modern Gaṅgā (Garhgaṅgā) being close to each other, the origin of Siwalik Sarasvatī (lost Sarasvatī) and Gaṅgā was recognised as one and the same. The origin of the last phase of Himalayan ranges or Siwalik ranges started around 2,00,00,000 years ago or in *Tretā yuga* of the 24th *Mahāyuga* of *Vaivasvata Manvantara*. This period was, as stated earlier, close to Rama's period, which is also described in *Purāṇas* as the 24th *Tretā*. We find the mention of Sarayū river during Rama's period and the same river has been mentioned in the list of rivers considered to have belonged to Siwalik phase by the present author. Thus the authenticity of the above discussion is also upheld by the mention of Sarayū in Rama's period which goes as far back as the origin of the last phase of Himalayas. As it has already been clarified that during the last phase of the origin of Himalayas, several new rivers issued from the mountain ranges that originated very late. Their names have also been cited as Saryū, Devikā, Kuhu, Gomatī, Dṛṣadvatī, Kauśikī, Tridivā, Niṣṭhivī, Gaṇḍakī, Cakṣu and Lohita etc. All of these rivers undoubtedly originated 2,00,00,000 years ago, the fact has also been born out by the mention of Saryū during Rama's period which without any shadow of doubt belonged to 2,00,00,000 years ago.

7

Dṛṣdvatī

When we take up the issue of Sarasvatī, Dṛṣdvatī cannot be left unmentioned. Dṛṣdvatī had a close connection with Sarasvatī during the Himalayan phase. As a result of origin of the last phase of Himalayas, Dṛṣdvatī originated from Yamunā. In fact, Yamunā's old course parted into two streams. The old stream came to be known as Sarasvatī and parted and newly emerged stream came to be known as Dṛṣ dvatī. Present day Dṛṣdvatī represents Chautang and Sarasvatī represents Mārkaṇḍā and Ghaggar. The upper stream is known as Mārkaṇḍā and lower stream as Ghaggar. Dṛṣdvatī flowed to the south of Kurukshetra and Sarasvatī to the north of Kurukshetra. This fact has been made clear by the following statement of *Vanaparva* of *Mahābhārata* (83.4)

> *dakṣiṇena sarasvatyā dṛṣdvatyuttareṇa ca ye vasanti kuruksetre te vasanti triviṣṭape.*

Since it was only the river that was prominently discernible in the region of Kurukshetra. It was known as Dṛṣdvatī. Here one thing may be remembered that by the time of origin of Dṛṣadvatī as a result of the diversion of Yamunā, the actual Sarasvatī, whose origin was associated with Gaṅgā, was no longer in existence. The Vedic Sarasvatī's stream, as stated earlier, ran through *Plakṣa* (modern Pilakhua) to *Vinaśana* (area adjoining modern Bisan near Beri in Rohtak district). The direction of this stream was to the east of Kuru region. So the actual Sarasvatī came to be known as eastern Sarasvatī in the plains. Its absence was also registered at Kurukshetra, Prabhāsa and Puṣkara by *Skanda Purāṇa* as under:

yadetad bhavatā proktaṁ prācī durlabhā viśeṣeṇa kurukshetre prabhāse puskare tathā.

Thus due to the absence of actual Sarasvatī in this region, the Yamunā's old stream called Mārkaṇḍā (named after Mārkaṇḍeya Muni) was taken for Sarasvatī by Mārkaṇḍeya Muni.

According to *Bṛhannāradīya Purāṇa's* memoirs, Mārkaṇḍeya Muni, seeing the absence of Sarasvatī in this region, observed penance to please the same. It is further narrated that having pleased with the Muni's prayers and penance the *Plakṣa* born Sarasvatī reached all those places where did the Muni observe penance. It also went westward after crossing the Sannihita Sara at Kurukshetra

sarasvatī mārkaṇḍeyena muninā saṁtaptam
paramaṁ tapaḥ tatra tatra samāyāta plakṣajātā
sā sabhājya stutā tena muninā dhārmikeṇa ha
saraḥ sannihitaṁ plāvya paścimaṁ prasthitā diśam
(64.17-18)

From the foregoing statement of the *Bṛhannāradīya Purāṇa*, it is clear that Mārkaṇḍā's origin is connected with Mārkaṇḍeya Muni when he declared southern stream of Yamunā as Sarasvatī.

Vāmana Purāṇa (37.16-23) also retains the same fact in its memory. Accordingly, Pitāmbara and Mārkaṇḍeya Ṛṣis fetched the river Sarasvatī from Svarga to Kurukshetra and Puṣkara for the welfare of humans. This was the reason why the Mārkaṇḍā was later associated with Sarasvatī. Thus the presently known river Sarasvatī rises from Sirmur area of Siwalik hills and enters the plains of Adibadri in Ambala district. It is joined by river Ghaggar near Shatrana in Patiala Dist. The combined river Sarasvatī\Ghaggar is lost in the desert a little west of Sirsa. Since Sarasvatī rises from the southern side of Siwalik hills, it carries water only during the rainy season. The present river cannot, therefore, be the old river Sarasvatī which was a mighty and holy river of India.

As stated earlier Mārkaṇḍā originated as the past stream

of Yamunā. In fact Yamunā was also the river that used to flow southward earlier. The very name Yamunā is a pointer to the fact that its flow was towards Yama (south) direction. *Yātrā parva* of *Mahābhārata* (chapter 9, verse 3) also informs that Yamunā used to flow towards the sea at the Kāmyaka vana, which was situated at the western boundary of Kurukshetra.

kāmyakaṁ nāma dadṛsurvanam munijanapriyam
smudragā mahāvegā yamunā yatra pāṇḍava.

In fact, the southern flow of Yamunā, which was known as western Sarasvatī or Mārkaṇḍā used to merge with Dṛṣ dvatī or modern Ghaggar at Pṛthūdaka. History tells us that Pṛthu of Venya performed a rite at this point of confluence. The very name Pṛthudaka or modern Pehova also indicates a point where does *pṛthaka* (separate) *udaka* (stream) mix up. This southern stream of Yamunā was also called Aruṇā.

The chemical examination of the waters of Mārkaṇḍā and Ghaggar have also shown the similarity of their waters with Yamunā.

Harivaṁsa Purāṇa (46.29-52) also mentions the diversion in the course of Yamunā. There a story has been narrated which shows Balarāma diverting the route of sea-going Yamunā towards Vṛndāvana with the help of his *Hala.*

rāmastu yamunāmāha snātumicche mahānadī
ehi māmapi gaccha tvaṁ rūpiṇī sāgaragame

In later periods due to some geological reasons, it seems that Yamunā also diverted its track towards the east and submerged itself into the basin of Gaṅgā at Prayāga. While etymologizing Yamunā, Yāska points out that Yamunā never had its independent flow, rather it submerges itself into the basin of some other river. This etymology clearly fixes the time period of Yāska after the period of Yamunā's diversion towards east and diversion also caused old stream named as Mārkaṇḍā go dry and so it became the rain-fed river considered to be originating from Adibadri of Sirmaur hills of Ambala Dist. The perennial flow of the river came to an end leaving its remnants in the forms of chows. The existence of various chows in the river basin was known as *Camsodbheda*, i.e. the origin of the river from *chamas* or chows. The chows of rain fed rivers can still be located in the region of Punjab and Haryana. Thus the reduction of perennial flow of the river into chow was known as *Camsodbheda. Camsodbheda* was not a geographical name, where from the Sarasvatī originated, but it referred to the remnants of the river into the forms of chows as discussed above.

8

The Yamuna as Sarasvatī

From the foregoing discussion it can be maintained that presently known Sarasvatī, i.e. Mārkaṇḍā and Ghaggar were once the old streams of southward flowing Yamunā (present Mārkaṇḍā and Ghaggar) which was known as western Sarasvatī or Dṛṣdvatī. Its eastward flowing sub-stream was known as Kālindi river.

In fact, the river Yamunā emerged from *Yamunotrī* glacier (the degenerated form of *Yamunāvataraṇam*) which is recognised in the *Purāṇas* as *Yamunā tīrtha*. Since this place was the partition point of two streams of Yamunā (main stream flowing southward was known as Yamunā, Kālindi, Hindon, Kālī *Nadī*, etc.), it was known as Tirtha. During *Mahābhārata* times also the southward flow of Yamunā was known as Sarasvatī. That is why *Vanaparva* (129.13) of *Mahābhārata* describes Yamunā Tirtha as *Plakṣāvataraṇam* which clearly points out to the fact that Yamunā Tirtha has become the place of rising of *Plakṣa*.

During *Mahābhārata* period eastern flow of Yamunā was a small stream since most of the waters of Yamunā were driven by the southward stream. This is supported by many historical facts. It is mentioned in *Srimadbhāgavat* that when Krishna was born in Mathura, his father Vasudeva took him across the river to Gokula where Nanda and mother Yaśodā lived. It is mentioned that at that time river was flooded. (Sri Krishna's birthday, *Janam aṣṭamī* always falls in the month of August which was the beginning of the rainy season by that time if calculated taking the time of precession accurately). Vasudeva waded across the river. Only at one point, the river water touched the feet of the child Krishna. This indicates that the river was just a small stream. Had it been the big river like the Yamunā of today with all water flowing through it, it would have been impossible for Vasudeva to cross it without using a boat or swimming. This makes one thing clear that the waters flowing through the present river Yamunā were not flowing through its present channel at that time.

Also, it may be known that during *Mahābhārata* Period, there was no big stream to the North of Indraprastha (present Delhi). This is supported by the fact that Hastinapur (capital of Kauravas) was located in the area of present Gaṅgā Yamunā doab. Kurukshetra, where the *Mahābhārata* battle was fought, is located to the west of the present river Yamunā. Thousands of soldiers and other people from Hastinapur went to Kurukshetra. Had there been a big river which they had to cross, there would have been an indication of this crossing in *Mahābhārata.* It is clear that there was no big river which the Kaurava armies had to cross to reach Kurukshetra

It seems that by the time of *Mahābhārata,* Yamunā started diverting its waters to the eastern stream. There is indication in *Mahābhārata* that during that time southern stream of Yamunā (or western Sarasvatī) had already started drying up at Kurukshetra, but at Pṛthudaka (present Pehova) it had ample water as king Yudhiṣṭhira performed the last rites of his relatives who had died in *Mahābhārata* at Pṛthudaka.

A Recent examination of archaeologists in this area has made it clear that there are a number of cities, which were neither destroyed by floods nor by human attacks. Kalibangan is one such place. Most probably these cities were abandoned because of the drying up of the river on the banks of which they had grown due to the shift of waters from the mainstream to the sub-stream. Their population also shifted to the northern and eastern parts of the country, which had ample rains, and the stream had ample water. Radiocarbon dating of the material recovered from Kalibangan has made it clear that the city was abandoned during 1800-1700

BC or 3700-3800 *Kali* era. Below the Harappan citadel of Kalibangan are the remains of the pre-Harappan township which was destroyed by an earthquake. Radiocarbon dating shows that the destruction of the town had taken place between 2450 and 2300 B.C. i.e. 700 and 800 *Kali* era. This indicates that the city and the fortress of Kalibangan were abandoned after they had been in existence for about 600 years. Thus most probably the shifting of Yamunā's waters from its southward flowing mainstream (Sarasvatī) to eastward flowing sub-stream (Kālindi) had started during *Mahābhārata* period, i.e. 5138 years ago.

Geographic and sedimentological evidence are also now available to make it clear that southward main course (known as Kālindi or Yamunā) were deriving the water from the one and same channel. The sedimentological evidence consists of the discovery of coarse greyish sand very similar in mineral content to that found in the bed of eastward flow of present Yamunā and in the boreholes in the southern bed at Kalibangan, situated near the present town of Hanumangarh in Gaṅgānagar district of Rajasthan. Eleven meters below the present flood level one found clay and silt deposits which are the result of the deposit of sand and silt brought down by the floodwaters of mainstream of Yamunā (Sarasvatī) during the past thousands of years.

Sarasvatī at confluence

The above discussion would help one unravel the mystery of Sarasvatī's presence at the confluence in Prayāga or Sarasvatī's capture by Gaṅgā. With the diversion of Yamunā's waters towards the east, the southern stream (Sarasvatī) had to go dry and it was stated that Sarasvatī was captured by Gaṅgā at Allahabad through Yamunā and so Allahabad came to be known as the meeting point of three rivers.

9

Kurukshetra

Kurukshetra was not the name of present day small city only, rather it was a big area often sandwiched between eastern Sarasvatī emerging from Pilakhua of UP and terminating at *Vinaśana* or modern Bisan in Rohtak and western Sarasvatī or modern Mārkaṇḍā and Ghaggar. Since it got infixed between the two rivers, it was called as Vedī (*Tāṇḍya Br.* quoted by C.V.Vaidya, P.70-72). This region of Kurukshetra was also known as Brahamāvarta. According to Manusmṛti, the place between Sarasvatī and Dṛṣdvatī was called Brahmāvart.

sarasvatī dṛṣadvatyor yadantaraṁ taṁ devanirmitaṁ desaṁ brahmāvarta pracakṣate.

As discussed above Kurukshetra was a vast region. We are told in the *Vanaparva* of *Mahābhārata* (83-84 chapters) that there were about 113 *tīrthas* included in this region known to the author of *Mahābhārata* the most striking feature is that among the *tīrthas* mentioned in Kurukshetra region, Gaṅgādvāra, modern Hardwar or Garhgaṅgā, the place of confluence of Gaṅgā and Sarasvatī have also been enumerated at serials 96 and 104 respectively in the list enclosed herewith. Moreover, the names like Sapta Gaṅgā and Yamunā prabhava tīrtha, etc. appear at the serial nos. 97 to 109. This clearly shows that limits of Kurukshetra region were up to Hardwar in the north. Here it may also be informed that *Plakṣa* has also been enumerated at serial no. 91 in the same list, which shows that *Plakṣa* was somewhere close to Gaṅgādvāra, i.e. Hardwar or Garhgaṅgā listed at serial no. 96. This fact also proves the present author's hypothesis that *Plakṣa* was modern Pilakhua which is very much close to Garhgaṅgā. List of *tīrthas* of Kurukshetra enumerated in *Vanaparva* of *Mahābhārata* is appended below:

1. Sannihita Sara-*Mahābhārata*, 83.10
2. Pariplva-ibid.83.12
3. Pṛthivī -ibid.83.13
4. Śālūkinī-ibid.83.13
5. Daśāśvamedha-ibid 83.14
6. Sarpadevī -83.14
7. Pañcanadam -83.16
8. Aśvin-83.17
9. Varāh-83.18
10. Somatīrtha-83.19
11. Ekahaṁśa-83.20
12. Kṛtasaucī-83.21
13. Muñjavaṭasthāna of Mahātmā Sthāṇu-83.22
14. Yakṣiṇī tīrtha-83.23
15. Rāmahrada (Paraśurāma Kuṇḍa)-83.26
16. Śri tīrtha-83.46
17. Kapila tīrtha-83-47
18. Sūrya-tīrtha-83.48
19. Gomavana-83.50
20. Śaṁkhinī-83.51
21. Arantuka-83.52
22. Brhmāvartta-83.53
23. Sutīrtha-83.54
24. Ambumatī-83.56

25. Kāśīśvara-83.57
26. Sitāvana-83.58
27. Nareśvara ṣ83.60
28. Śvāvillopāmaha-83.61
29. Daśāsvamedha-83.64
30. Mānuśa tīrtha-83.66
31. Apagā Nadī, one krośa east to the Mānuśa tīrtha.-83.67
32. Brahmodumbara-83.71
33. Saptarṣi kuṇḍa-83.72
34. Kedāra tīrtha-83.72
35. Kapila kedāra-83.73
36. Sāraka tīrtha-83.75
37. Iḷaspada tīrtha-83.77
38. Kiṁdāna kiṁjipya-83.79
39. Kalaśī tīrtha-83.80
40. Nārada's birth in the form of Ambā-83.81
41. Puṇḍrīka-83.83
42. Triviṣṭap tīrtha-83.84
43. Falakīvana-83.86
44. Dṛṣdvatī-83.87
45. Sarvadevī-83.88
46. Pāṇikhāta-83.89
47. Miśraka-83.91
48. Vyāsavana-83.93
49. Madhuvaṭī-83.94
50. Confluence of Kauśikī and Mārkaṇḍā-83.95

51. Vyāsa sthali-83.96
52. Ahan-sudina-83.100
53. Mṛgadhūma tīrtha (where people go to take a dip into Gaṅgā)-83.101
54. Vāmana tīrtha-83.103
55. Pavana hrada-Amara hrada-83.104,105
56. Śālihotra-83.107
57. Srikuñja named Sarasvatī tīrtha-83.108
58. Naimiṣa kuñja-83.109
59. Kanyā tīrtha-83.112
60. Brahmatīrtha-83.113
61. Soma tīrtha-83.114
62. Saptasārasvata-83.115
63. Auśanasa-83.135
64. Kapālamocana-83.137
65. Agni tīrtha-83.138
66. Brhmayoni tīrtha-83.139
67. Pṛthudak-83.141
68. Madhusrva-83.150
69. Confluence of Sarasvatī and Aruṇā-83.151
70. Ardha kīla-83.153
71. Śatasahasra and Sāhsraka-83.158
72. Reṇukā tīrtha-83.160
73. Vimocana-83.161
74. Pañcavaṭī-83.162
75. Taijasa named Varuṇa-83.164
76. Kurutīrtha east of Taijasa-83.165

77. Svastipura-83.174
78. Pavana tīrtha-83.175
79. Gaṅga hrada-83.177
80. Āpgā-83.177
81. Sthāṇuvaṭa-83.178
82. Badaripācana Vaśiṣṭhāśram-83.179
83. Ekarātra tīrtha-83.182
84. Trailokya tīrtha-83.183
85. Dadhīca tīrtha-83.186
86. Kanyāśrama-83.189
87. Sannihita tīrtha-83.190
88. Dvārapāla Mayakrukam-83.200
89. Koṭi tīrtha-83.202
90. Samantapañcaka-83.208
91. Plakṣa-84.62
92. Śatakumbhā, Pañcayajñā
93. Triśūla khāt
94. Śākambharī
95. Suvarṇa tīrtha-84-19
96. Gaṅgādvara-84.26
97. Saptagaṅgā, Trigaṅgā and Śakrāvarta-84.29
98. Kapilavaṭa-84.31
99. Nāgatīrtha-84.33
100. Santanuka lalitaka-84.34
101. Confluence between Gaṅgā and Yamunā-84.35
102. Sugandhā-84.36
103. Rudrāvarta-84.37

104. Confluence of Gaṅgā and Sarasvatī-84.38
105. Bhadrakaṇeśvara-84.39
106. Kubjabhraka-84.40
107. Samudraka close to Arundhatī vaṭa-84.42
108. Brhmāvarta tīrtha-84.43
109. Yamunā prabhava tīrtha-84.44
110. Origin of Sindhu-84.46
111. Vedī tīrtha-84.47
112. Vāsiṣṭhī-84.48
113. Bhṛgu tuṅga-84.49

10

Sarasvatī during Rāmāyaṇa Period

It is mentioned in *Vālmīki Rāmāyaṇa* that when king Daśaratha died Śri Rama and Lakṣamaṇa had already left Ayodhyā and Bharata and Śatrughna were with their maternal grandparents in Kekaya, the area between the two rivers Sindhu and Jehlum. The couriers from Ayodhyā crossed river Gaṅgā and its tributaries and passed through Kurujāṅgala, an area having a large number of lotus pools and streams and reached river Dṛṣadvatī (Chautang). They crossed river Ikṣ umatī that also flowed near Kurukshetra and near Śairiṣika (Modern Sirsa). They moved westward and crossed river Vipāsa (Beas) near the holy place Viṣṇupāda. After crossing a number of other streams and passing through forests they reached the city of Girivarja, the capital of Kekayas. On the return journey, Bharata and his escorts took a much northerly course near the foothills. While describing the return journey of prince Bharata from Girivarja in Kekaya to Ayodhyā, *Vālmīki Rāmāyaṇa* (Baroda, 1962, *Ayodhyā Kāṇḍa* 65.1-10) refers to his crossing joint stream of Sarasvatī and Gaṅgā before entering Bhāruṇḍa forest in the north of *Kīra-Matsya*s. The above description of Rāmāyaṇa clearly lays down the position of Sarasvatī some two crore years ago at the time of origin of the last phase of Himalayan mountains. The situation of rivers as described in Rāmāyaṇa clearly indicates that Dṛṣdvatī at that time was located to the east of Kurukshetra, which is surely the present Chautang. Ghaggar was called Ikṣumatī and it also used to flow close to Kurukshetra towards down south. Sarasvatī and Gaṅgā are described as joint streams. This also supports the Puranic view that Sarasvatī and Gaṅgā considered having originated from one and the same place after the origin of upper Himalayan ranges took place and this situation continued to persist till the period of Rāmāyaṇa i.e. two crore years ago, the time of origin of last phase of Himalayan mountains. This joint stream undoubtedly existed somewhere near Pilakhua or Garhgaṅgā. From this point onward Sarasvatī and Gaṅgā must have parted their streams. It is also mentioned that after crossing the joint streams Bharata entered the Bhāruṇḍa forest of *Kīra-Matsya*s. The Bhāruṇḍa forest was nothing else but the area of present Baraut. So it is the established fact that till the time of Rāmāyaṇa, Sarasvatī considered having originated from the original source of Gaṅgā itself. The waters of Gaṅgā and Yamunā have respectively been discriminated as white and black. Sarasvatī is endowed with the attributive epithet of whiteness. So its ancient link with Gaṅgā can not be disputed. Later when the last phase of Himalayan mountains was concluding its origin, Sarasvatī's parted stream diverted to join with Gaṅgā herself and so due to the non-availability of Sarasvatī, Yamunā was looked upon as Sarasvatī. This is why the place of *Plakṣa* was described to have replaced Yamunā tīrtha. (*plakṣāvataraṇam yamunātīrtham*).

In fact, the stream of Sarasvatī emerging from Gaṅgā at Pilakhua was again called as Prācī Sarasvatī and it flowed through Brahmāvartta, Devamārga and Puṣkara.

snātvā śudhimavāpnoti yatra prācī sarasvatī
devamārgapratiṣṭhā yā devamārgeṇa niḥsṛtā
(*Vāmana Purāṇa*, 21.19)

athādikṣata rājā tu haya medha śatena saḥ
brahmāvarte manoḥ kṣetre yatra prācī sarasvatī
(*Bhāgvata Purāṇa*, 4.19.1)

puṣkrāraṇyamāsādya prācīyatra sarasvatī
matiḥ smṛtiḥ śubhā prajñā medhābudhiryā parā
sarasvatyās tu paryāyāṣṣaḍete saṁprakīrtitiāḥ
tataḥ prabhṛti yatrāsau prācībh ūtā sarasvatī
(*Padma Purāṇa*, *Sṛṣṭikhaṇḍa*,18.220-221)

11

Sarasvatī during Mahābhārata Period

The most recent memory of Sarasvatī is registered in the records of *Mahābhārata* epic. This record dates back to 5000 years. Thus on the basis of references occurred in *Mahābhārata,* one can easily draw the picture of the existence of Sarasvatī 5000 years ago. One such reference is Balarāma's *Pratisrota yātrā* of Sarasvatī or voyage of Sarasvatī from its terminus to the source. With the help of the account of Balarāma's voyage; one can easily explore the whereabouts of Sarasvatī's flow 5000 years ago since Balarāma is said to have travelled from terminus to source.

11.1 Prabhāsa:

As per records of *Mahābhārata,* Balarāma started his journey from the terminus of Sarasvatī and that terminus is mentioned as Prabhāsa. Prabhāsa was situated at the seacoast. Dvārakā was established in the region of Prabhāsa. Due to the extension of the desert, the area of Prabhāsa also got extended. 5000 years ago, the present day Pāṭan was the Prabhāsa region. Pāṭan was considered to be the terminus of Sarasvatī during *Mahābhārata* period.

11.2 Camsodbheda

It was considered to be the next southward point of Sarasvatī's existence 5000 years ago. Camasodbheda was not some particular place, as is often considered by many of the present day historians and archaeologists, rather it represented the dried-up riverbed of Sarasvatī in the form of a chow or a rainfed stream. Here it may also be clarified that *udbheda* often denotes the origin of a river, e.g. *Gaṅgodbheda* denotes the origin of Gaṅgā river. *Camasodbheda* denotes the emergence of chows in the old dried up riverbed of Sarasvatī. This *Camasodbheda* most likely is represented by modern Chambal river. It is clear from the above reference that till the time of *Mahābhārata* or 5000 years ago Sarasvatī was not in existence, rather its remnants in the form of chows in the dried up bed were in existence. The combined name of these chows later came to be known as Chambal.

11.3 Udpāna

Was a well next to the original source of famous *chamas* or modern Chambal river in the dried up riverbed of Sarasvatī.

11.4 Vinaśana

Vinaśana was the place where did Sarasvatī go dry. It did not denote a particular point in the desert of Rajasthan and Gujrat, but the whole region from Udpāna onward till Bisan of Rohtak in Haryana fall within the range of *Vinaśana*. We have already given a detailed discussion regarding the possible location of *Vinaśana*.

11.5 Subhūmika

Subhūmika was a place in Kurukshetra near Pehova where Sarasvatī (Mod. Mārkaṇḍā) and Dṛṣdvatī (modern Ghaggar) used to mix up. This region was dominated by various classes of Devas, Gandharvas, and Rakṣasas.

11.6 Gandharva tīrtha, Gargastrota, Śaṇatīrtha

Gandharva tīrtha, Gargastrota and Śaṇatīrtha were also various places situated in Kuru region. Their actual location is not known today. But it cannot be gainsaid that these places were not far from Subhūmika, which was inhabited by Gandharvas and others.

11.7 Dvaitasara

Dvaitasara is also mentioned as situated in the course of

Sarasvatī, but their location couldn't be identified today. In fact, all these places were situated along the dried up bed of Sarasvatī. Dvaitasara may be located in the name of Dasaur, etc.

11.8 Nāgadhanvana

Sarasvatī is said to have turned from south to eastward at this point

11.9 Naimiṣāraṇya

According to *Vāyu Purāṇa* (1.14) Naimiṣāraṇya was situated on the banks of river Dṛṣadvatī or modern Chautang. *Purāṇas* were written on this spot. The area of modern Nimsāra lying in district of Sitapur of UP situated on the banks of Gomati identified as ancient Naimiṣa tīrtha cannot be the Naimiṣāraṇya of Kurukshetra region. In fact the area between Naimiṣāraṇya and Samantapañcaka was known as Saṁnyāsī region in the period of *Mahābhārata.*

According to *Āraṇyakaparva* (81.178), Samantapañcaka was situated to the south of Sarasvatī and north of Dṛṣadvatī. Thus Samantapañcaka was considered to be an area adjoining Kurukshetra where Oghavatī flowed. The southern and northern region of Sarasvatī near Kurukshetra has also been called Samantapañcaka which was considered as a sacred tīrtha due to Paraśurāma who filled five ponds with the blood of Kṣatriyas and thus satisfied the souls of his ancestors.

sametānām anto yasmin tat saman

(*Ādiparva*, 2.8-11, *Mahābhārata*)

11.10 Saptasārasvata

This place was situated on the bank of Sarasvatī. It was so named because of the presence of Badrī, Iṅguda, Plakṣa, Aśvatha, Palāśa, Karīra, and Pilu trees. The above seven types of trees were the conspicuous features of relief on the banks of Sarasvatī. It was full of birds and very often visited by saints.

11.11 Maṅkaṇaka Aśrama

Maṅkaṇaka Āśrama was situated in the area of Saptasārasvata only.

saptasārasvatam tīrtham tato gacchennarādhipa

yatra maṅkaṇakaḥ siddho maharṣi lokaviśrutaḥ

(*Mahābhārata* Vana*parva* 83.175)

11.12 Uśanasa or Kapālamocana Tīrtha

This tīrtha is close to Sannihita sarovara.

11.13 Ṛṣṇu Āśrama

Here Viśvāmitra, Sindhudvīpa and Devāpi named kings attained Brāhmaṇaship.

11.14 Pṛthudaka

Pṛthudaka is modern Pehova. This place is famous for the confluence of Aruṇā and Sarasvatī.

11.15 Ārṣṭiṣena Āśrama, Daṇḍaka-vana, Yāyāta, Vaśiṣṭha flow

At Sthāṇu tīrtha on the eastern side of Sarasvatī was the hermitage of Vasiṣṭha. Similarly, western side had the hermitage of Viśvāmitra.

11.16 Soma Tīrtha, Brahmayonī

This place had the forest of Kuber, the leader of Yakṣ as.

11.17 Badripācana

This place witnessed the 12 years' long famine. During famine, the residents of Badripācana set out in search of foodgrains for the Himalayas leaving Arundhatī. Vasiṣṭha Āśrama is also situated at this place. In fact, this place was also close to Thāneśwara.

11.18 Śukra Tīrtha

Śukra tīrtha is situated near Oghavatī in Kurukśetra region.

11.19 Yamunā Tīrtha

Yamunā tīrtha is most probably modern Yamunānagar or Yamunottrī where does Yamunā issue from.

11.20 Sārasvata Tīrtha

This place was close to Badripācana, since it was also affected by the 12 years' famine. This tīrtha was named after a Sārasvata Ṛṣi who used to impart the knowledge of Vedas to the Vedic students and scholars.

11.21 Samantapañcaka and Kurukshetra

The region between Rāmasarovara, popularly known as Ramarāpiṇḍārā near Jind in modern times, and Macakruka sarovara and Tarantuka and Arantuka were known as Kurukshetra.

tarantukārantukayor yad antaram
rāmahṛdānām ca macakrukasya ca
etat kurukṣetram samantapañcakam
pit asahasyottaravedir ucyate

(*Mahābhārata Vanaparva,*83.208)

Samantapañcaka was also situated at a place where Sarasvatī flowed in the name of Oghavatī. Oghavatī has been described as a tributary of Sarasvatī in *Śalya parva* of *Mahābhārata* (*Geog. of Mahābhārata* P.133).

11.22 Plakṣa Prasravaṇa

This was the source of Sarasvatī in Brāhmaṇic period. Here ended the terminus to source voyage of Balarāma. After Yudhiṣṭhira Kurujāṅgala and Sarasvatī region fall in the domain of Prikṣita second. We have already had a lot of discussion on this issue in the foregoing pages. It has been established that Plakṣa was Pilakhua of western UP.

12

Some Aspects of Sarasvatī

12.1 Sarasvatī as mighty river

The Paurāṇika tradition has quoted Sarasvatī, not as a rainfed river but a great river having its perennial flow.

varṣākāla vahāḥ sarvā varjayitvā sarasvatīm
(*Vāmana Purāṇa*, 34.8)

In fact all other rivers have been described as rain fed river. The description of Purāṇas legalizes the Vedic description of Sarasvatī, as the mother of rivers.

āyat sākaṁ yaśso vāvaśānāḥ
sarasvatīsaptathī sindhumātā
yāsuṣvamanta sudhughāḥ sudhārāḥ
abhisvena payasā pīnvamānāḥ

12.2 Sarasvatī out side India

Mention of Sarasvatī has been made in the old scriptures of Parsis (Avesta) as Haraharavati. Parsis are Indians who migrated around 2,00,000 years ago. Sarasvatī is known as Helmond in Afghanistan and Auragothi in Assyrian, which indicates that Assyria, is populated with the people of India who migrated from Kurukshetra. Sarasvatī in Kurukshetra is known as Aughavati. Auragothi of Assyria is a corruption of Aughavatī that has been introduced by Indians migrated to Assyria thousands of years ago.

12.3 Withdrawing of Western Sea

Mahābhārata Clearly mentions that desert of Rajasthan

and Gujrat came into being due to withdrawing of sea. By the time of withdrawing of sea, Sarasvatī was not flowing through the desert. That is why, Utathya has shown praying to Sarasvatī that it should go through the desert underground or unseen because her absence rendered this country worthless.

tatastadiriṇaṁ jātaṁ samudrasyāvar sarpataḥ
tasmād deśān nadīṁcaivaprovācāsau dvijottamaḥ
adṛśyā gaccha bhīrū tvaṁ sarasvatī marun prati
apuṇya eṣa bhavatu deśastyaktastvayā śubhe
(*Mahābhārata Anuśāsana Parva*, 154.26-27)

13

Sarasvatī and Gaṅgā

Origin of Sarasvatī and Gaṅgā has been described as one and same by the tradition of *Brahmavaivarta Purāṇa.*

13.1 Sequence of Gaṅgā Yamunā and Sarasvatī

As per the tradition of *Yogaśāstra,* Sarasvatī got sandwiched between Gaṅgā in the eastern side and Yamunā in the western side.

iḍā bhāgīrathī gaṅgā piṅgalā yamunā nadī
tayormadhyagatā nādīsuṣumnārūpā sarasvatī

This evidence clearly proves Sarasvatī's link with Gaṅgā at the spot of their origins. This also supports the viewpoint of Gaṅgā-Sarasvatī-Saṅgama, which has been described as one of the Tīrtha's lying in the Kurukshetra region. Tīrtha, in fact, was a place of confluence of two rivers.

13.2 Sarasvatī's origin from Gaṅgā

In *Āraṇyaka parva* of *Rāmāyaṇa* a reference has been made about Gaṅgā, according to which after coming down from heaven to Earth, Gaṅgā got divided into seven channels (*Āryaṇyaka Parva* 109,10-12. BORI)

The *Rāmāyaṇa* more clearly maintains that Śiva brought Gaṅgā and left loose her in Bindu sarovar, from there it got divided into seven streams (*Rāmā.*1.42.6, Oriental Institute of Baroda) According to the reference of *Ādiparva* of *Mahābhārata,* Gaṅgā emerged out of the golden peak (Hemakūṭa) of Gaṅgotrī in the Himalayas, got divided into seven channels and ultimately merged into sea. (*Ādiparva,* 169.19-20; 196.11). These seven channels are known as

Viśvokasārā, Nalinī, Pāvanī, Sarasvatī, Jāmu Nadī, Sitā, Gaṅgā and Sindhu (*Bhiṣma parva*, 6.7.45 BORI, 6.6.98 Garahhpur). Out of the above mentioned channels, Sarasvatī disappears at some places and reappears at another place (*Bhiṣmaparva*, 6.6.47, also *Geog. of Mahābhārata*, 1986: 127)

In fact, the foregoing description reveals that Sarasvatī lost its existence after the rise of the last phase of Himalayan mountains completed and since then it came to be associated with Gaṅgā only. *Rāmāyaṇa* has also mentioned its origin from Gaṅgā. The Rāmāyaṇa's period also goes back to the period of origin of the last phase of Himalayan ranges i.e. 2 crore years ago.

In the Vedic period the case was not so. There it was known as the seventh mother of six rivers:

saptathī sindhumātā (RV)

VS. (34.11) mentions Sarasvatī as having its five tributaries.

pañcnadhyaḥ sarasvatīmaapiyanti sasrotasaḥ
sarasvatī tu pañcadhā sodeśe'bhavat sarit

Thus during the Himalayan period, Sarasvatī was an independent mighty river or *Nadītamā*.

ambitame naditame sarasvatī (*RV*. 2.41.16)

It was only during the Himalayan phase that it came to be recognised as the tributary of Gaṇgā. This was the reason that it was revoked as forming *Triveṇī* at Allahabad in the company of Gaṅgā. Folktales of the people of Mana village in the Garhwal Himalayas also go in the support of this fact.

13.3 Delinking of Sarasvatī from Gaṅgā

The description of *Brahmavaivarta Purāṇa*, which goes as far back as 20 to 40 lakh years ago, clearly records the event of the abandonment of Gaṅgā Sarasvatī. According to the description of the *Purāṇa*, Gaṅgā, Lakṣmī and Sarasvatī were spouses of Nārāyaṇa.

lakṣmīsarasvatī tisro bhāryā harerapi
(*Brahmavaivarta Pu.* 11, Ch. 6.17)

The Same type of description is traceable in *Devībhāgavata* (2.9.6.17) as below:

lakṣmī sarasvatī gaṅgā tisro bhāryā harerapi
premṇā samastāstiṣṭhanti satataṁ hari sannidhau

This, in fact, is an allegorical description where Nārā are the waters and Nārāyaṇa is the base of water. It is clear from the following statements.

āpo vai nārā proktā āpo vai narasūnavaḥ
tadasya yadāyatanaṁ nārāyaṇaṁ smṛtaṁ

The story of *Brahmavaivarta Purāṇa* further holds that there arose a dispute between Gaṅgā and Sarasvatī in which both exchanged curses leading to pledge by Gaṅgā to end Sarasvatī's existence. (*Brahmavaivarta Purāṇa* (Chapter 6.70-71).

This story is indicative of the fact that Gaṅgā Sarasvatī dried up or submerged itself into the basin of Gaṅgā due to some tectonic seismic volcanic upheaval.

After the Gaṅgā Sarasvatī came to an end. Sarasvatī finds its new emergence in the holy land of Bharata as Yamunā and Sarasvatī. The *Purāṇa* tells us that as decreed by Nārāyaṇa the Sarasvatī cursed by Gaṅgā to turn black descended on the holy place of Bhārata which undoubtedly is Kurukshetra.

puṇyakṣetre hyājagāma bhārate sā sarasvatī
gaṅgā śāpena kalayā svayaṁ tasthau hare

(*Brahmavaivarta Pu.* 2.7.1)

Gaṅgā's curse to blacken Sarasvatī clearly reveals the fact that after severing its links from Gaṅgā, Sarasvatī emerged from Yamunā whose waters are thought to be black hued as compared to Gaṅgā.

14

Ikṣumatī as Ghaggar

As referred to above (Ch.12) the couriers from Ayodhyā on their way to Girivraj crossed Dṛṣadvatī (Chautang) afterwards they crossed Śaradaṇḍā (present Sadādenī a tributary of Mārkaṇḍā river and forded by them was Ikṣ umatī.

ajkūlāṁ tataḥ prāpya bodhīnām nagaraṁyayuḥ
pitṛpaitāmahīṁ puṇyāṁ terikṣumatīṁ nadīṁ

(*Ayodhyā Kāṇḍa*, 62.12)

Ikṣumatī can be identified with modern Ghaggar. *Mahābhārata* describes Ikṣumatī as the river of Kurukshetra.

kurukṣetraṁ ca vasatāṁ Nadīm ikṣumatīm anu
jaghanya jastalakaṣya śrutaseneti yaḥ śrutaḥ

(*Ādiparva*, 3.141)

Literally, the name Tkṣumati signifies a river rich in sugarcane or whose belt is particularly noteworthy for its cane crops. This is applicable only to present river Ghaggar that is called Hakra in Rajasthan.

In several villages in Parganas of Jodhpur and Malani in Rajasthan stone cane crushers were found by Gauri Shanker Hira Chand Ojha (1954) which were used for *Gur* or jaggery preparation where Hakra flowed. Sultan Masud son of Mahmud of Ghazni, found the track around the town of Sirsa remarkable for extensive growth of cane which his forces used to fill up the moat for storing the fortress. (*Indian Antiquary*, 1932: 61, P.164). The records of Timur's invasion also mention the sugarcane jungles of Tohana (*Indian Antiquary*, 1932: 61, P.164). Both the towns of Sirsa and Tohānā are situated near Ghaggar. In fact due to heavy sugarcane crops the river was called Ikṣumatī and the people who lived in this region were also known as Ikṣvākus. That is why Ikṣumatī has been attributed with the epithet of *pitṛpaitāmahī* which has apparently been defined by the commentators as connected with the ancestors of Ilkṣvākus. (*Rāmāyaṇa*, Gujrati Press, Vol. II. P. 803).

Thus by the time of *Rāmāyaṇa*, modern Ghaggar was famous as Ikṣumatī. From the foregoing discussion again it is clear that even by the period of *Rāmāyaṇa* Mārkaṇḍā and Ghaggar could not come to be known as Sarasvatī. Since Sarasvatī was maintaining its parted course from Gaṅgā. It was perhaps only around two crore years ago i.e. by the period of completion of Siwalik ranges that Gaṅgā Sarasvatī was completely abandoned and Yamunā Sarasvatī came into being.

15

Origin of Mārkaṇḍā And Abandonment of Sarasvatī

As the Paurāṇika records had it, the origin of Mārkaṇḍā owed to the diversion of Sarasvatī's waters in the beginning of *Vaivasvata Manvantara* i.e. 12 crore years ago, the time period of great deluge when Himalayan ranges began to form due to volcanic upheaval. In fact, Mārkaṇḍā emerged entirely as the new river in the process of diversion of Sarasvatī. According to the allegorical narrative of the *Purāṇas,* Sarasvatī on being propitiated agreed to follow the sage Mārkaṇḍeya.

pratyuvāca mahātmānaṁ mārkaṇḍeyaṁ mahāmunim
yatra tvaṁ neṣyase vipra tatra yāsyāmyatandratā

(*Vāmana Purāṇa*, 11.23)

Sage Mārkaṇḍeya is stated to have witnessed the great deluge in the age of *Vaivasvata Manu* (*Mahābhārata Vanaparva*, Chapters 186-187 and *Bhāgavata Purāṇa*, 12.8)

The reference clearly connects the diversion of Sarasvatī's waters 12 crore years ago in the age of *Vaivasvata Manu* when the great Deluge occurred and Himalayan ranges began to form. In fact, it was the formation of the Himalayan ranges that caused diversion of the perennial flow of Sarasvatī and the origin of Mārkaṇḍā as a result thereof.

Padma Purāṇa, Sṛṣṭi khaṇḍa (18.198) also informs that river Sarasvatī vanished underground on account of *Vaḍvānala* which carried it to the ocean. This reference of

Vaḍvānala also points out the period of *Vaivasvata Manu* when Himalayan ranges began to form due to tectonic-seismic-volcanic upheaval.

16

Places lying on the banks of Sarasvatī

16.1 Saurāṣtra, Sauvīra, Matsya and Kurujāṅgala

As per *Śri Madbhāgavata Purāṇa* (*Vidur Yātrā tīrtha, Vidur Saṁvād* Chap. 1 Verse 24), Saurāṣṭra, Sauvīr, Matsya and Kurujāṅgala regions were lying on the banks of the Sarasvatī. Kurujāṅgala was the region close to Yamunā.

tatastvati vrajya surāṣṭramṛddhaṁ sauvīra-matsyān
kurujāṅgalārca kālena tāvadyamun āmupetya
tatroddhavaṁ bhāgavataṁ dadarśa

16.2 Plakṣa, Ābu Parvat and Girnāra

Skand Purāṇa (7.33.40-41) mentions Sarasvatī's origin from Plakṣa, a place situated down the glacier.

tato visṛjya tāṁ deviṁ nadī bhūtvā sarasvatī
himvataṁ giriṁ prāpya plakṣāt tatra vinirgatā-40
avatīrṇā dharāpṛṣṭhe matsya-kacchapa saṁkulā-41

Skand Purāṇa (part 7 viz. *Prabhāsa khaṇḍa*, Chap. 35, *Sarasvatī Sagara Saṁgama* and *Agni Tīrtha Mahātmya*) mentions Sarasvatī passing near Ābu Parvat and then passing near Girnāra before merging with Sea. Near sea it is shown as splitting into five streams named as Hāriṇī, Vajriṇī, Nyaṁku, Kapilā and Sarasvatī.

16.3 Puṣkara, Kurukshetra

As per *Vāmana Purāṇa* (37. 16.23) for the well being of humans, Pitāmbara and Mārkaṇḍeya brought Sarasvatī from *Svarga* (upper Himalayas) to Puṣkara and Kurukshetra.

According to *Matsya Purāṇa* (186.10) also Sarasvatī flowed at Kurukshetra.

puṇyā kanakhale gaṅgā kurukshetre sarasvatī

grāme kā yadi vā'raṇye puṇā sarvatranarmadā

Thus during the period of origin of *Vāmana* and *Matsya Purāṇas* Sarasvatī flowed via Kurukshetra. Both of these *Purāṇas* belong to the same time frame.

16.4 Dvaitavana

At another place, *Vāmana Purāṇa* (3.4) refers to Sarasvatī's origin from Plakṣa and at the same time mentions that after passing through thousands of stones it entered the Dvaitavana.

plakṣa vṛkṣāt samudbhūtā saricchareṣṭā sanātanī
sarva pāpakṣya karīsmaraṇādapi nityaśaḥ
saiṣā śaila sahasrāṇi vidārya mahānadī
praviṣṭā puṇyatoyaiṣā vanaṁ dvaitamiti śrutam

Dvaitavana has been identified as Deobandh which is around 50 miles north of Meerut. So, if Pilakhua is taken as the source of Sarasvatī, the proposition of Dvaitavana as Deobandh comes true.

16.5 Naimiṣāraṇya, Camasodbheda, Śivodbheda and Nāgodbheda

As per records of *Vāyu Purāṇa* (1.14), Naimiṣāraṇya was located on the banks of river Dṛṣadvatī. The *Purāṇas* were written on this spot. In modern times Naimiṣāraṇya is located on the banks of Gomatī, in the modern district of Sitapur n UP. This makes it clear that by the time of origin of the tradition of *Vāyu Purāṇa*, Sarasvatī flowed via modern UP and must have appeared in the form of Camas river or modern Chambal which is popularly known in *Purāṇas* as

Camasodbheda. Thus by that time, Gomatī was Dṛṣadvatī. This fact also reflects ample good light on the chronology of *Purāṇas*. One may easily confer that tradition of *Vāyu Purāṇa* is much older than the traditions of *Vāmana* and *Matsya Purāṇas*.

According to the tradition of *Bṛhannāradīya Purāṇa* (64.17-18), Mārkaṇḍeya Muni did great penance for bringing the Sarasvatī down the *Plakṣa*. It followed all the points where penances were observed by Mārkaṇḍeya Muni. It flowed via Sannihita Sara which is evidently situated in Kurukshetra. Here the term penance signifies the efforts put in by sage to make the river flow.

mārkaṇḍeyena muninā saṁtaptaṁ paramaṁ tapaḥ
tatra tatra samāyātā plakṣajātā sarasvatī
sā sabhājya stutātena muninā dhārmikena ha
saraḥ sannihitaṁ plāvya paścimāṁ prasthitā diśam

On the basis of the above statements, it can be inferred that the bed of Sarasvatī laid through the places where Mārkaṇḍeya did penances.

As per records of *Mahābhārata* (*Vana Parva*, 82), Sarasvatī having lost in the sands reappeared at Camasodbheda, Śivodbheda and Nāgodbheda.

16.6 Sthāneśvara

It is said that an early king of Solar Dynasty King Ben got afflicted with leprosy. He was advised to perform penance on the bank of holy Sarasvatī. When he got cured he built Sthāneśvara temple on that spot. A town grew near the temple and was also called Sthāneśvara. Gradually its name changed to Thanesara, which is presently a part of Kurukshetra city.

16.7 Pehova

There is a mention of the river, Sarasvatī in *Mahābhārata*. When the battle of *Mahābhārata* was over, king Yudhiṣṭhira went to Pṛthudaka (present Pehova) on the banks of river Sarasvatī to perform last rights of those relatives killed in the battle. Even today this custom exists among the Hindus. The last right of the people who die a premature death or who die *avagat*, i.e. laying in bed or in accident etc. are still performed at Pehova. Most probably the river Sarasvatī had already dried up at Kurukshetra or had started flowing underground according to old Indian tradition, otherwise, it could have been possible for Yudhiṣṭ hira to perform last rites at Kurukshetra in the waters of Sarasvatī.

16.8 Vṛddhakanyāka, Sārasvata, Āditya, Tīrtha, Kauber, Vaijayantī and Vaṁśodbheda

Devala (quoted in *Kṛtya Kalpataru*, 1942: 250) describes Vṛddhakanyāka, Sārasvata, Āditya tīrtha, Kaubera, Vaijayantī, Pṛthūdaka, *Vinaśana*, Vaṁśodbheda, Prabhāsa, Naimiṣa *tīrthas* situated along the course of Sarasvatī.

plakṣ praśravaṇaṁ vṛddhkanyākaṁ sārasvatamāditya
īrthaṁ kauberaṁ vaijayantyam
pṛthūdakaṁ naimiṣaṁ vinaśanaṁ vaṁśodbhedaṁ
prabhāsamiti sārasvatāni

17

References of Sarasvatī in Sanskrit literature

17.1 References of Sarasvatī in Epics

Xkak; eqkpS Iy{kt kr kl jLorhe~
jFkL; kal j; aapS xkSr hax. Mdhar Fkk

(*Mahābhārata, Ādiparva,* 169.20)

r= i q; rjar hFkZ Iy {kkor j. ka' 'kqHke~
;= l kj Lor h "Vok xPNUR; oHkFkS; Z k%

(*MahÈbhÈrata, Vanaparva*, 90.4)

, r r~ Iy {kkor j . ka; eqkr hFkZ ekqHke~A
, r r~ oSukd i "BL; }kj ekgqZ hf'k k%AA

(*ibid.* 129.13)

"kkar kufHkok{ kFk i k' oZfge or ksP; q%
l U; kd k; kZ k l okZ k fuoR; kZ #gspy e~

(*Mahābharata, Śalyaparva*, 54.9)

ukfr nj qar r ksxR ok uxar ky /ot kscy h A

(*ibid.* 54.10)

i q; ar hFkZ j an"Vok foLe; ai j eaxr %A
i Hkoap l j LoR; k Iy {k i z o. kacy %AA

(*ibid.* 54.11)

l aHkr %d kj i ouai o j ar hFkZ qHke~A

(*Ibid.* 54.12)

l kSfUkd ouaj kt ar r ksxPNs ekuo%A

(*Mahābhārata, Vanaparva,* 84.4)

rr'pkfi l fjPN%Bkunhuke~qÙkekunh A

(*Ibid.* 84.6)

Iy{kknnsoh l qkjkt u~eghi q; kl jLorh A
Rk=kfHk'kd adqhZ cYehd kfUl%or st ysAA

(*ibid.* 84.7)

rFkkSr kcged U;sfr y{ehofUÙk%d jLorh A
n.Mulhfr t Z) k=hn.Mksg cgfpxzA

(*Mahābhārata, Śāntiparva,* 121.24)

Sarasvati is the first among these rivers that terminated into the sea in the Indian part of Globe.

, 'kkl jLorh i q; kunhukeqÙkekunh A
i Zekkl oZfj r kaunh l kxj xkfeuh AA

(*Mahābhārata, Anuśāsanaparva*, 134.15)

Udpāna was a well in the riverbed of Sarasvatī. This fact has been clarified in *Mahābhārata* as under:

mni kuap ran'Vok i žkL; p i q%i q%A
unhxr enhukRek i kr ksfou'kuar nk AA

(*Mahābhārata, Śalya parva*, 35.53)

Samantapañcaka at the banks of Sarasvatī :

rr %d qkjeknk; nsok cgei jqkxek%A
vfHk'kd kFkZk Xeq%ksl bhzal fgr kLr r %AA
i q; kagSor hanohal fjPN'Bkal jLor he~A
l eUri pd s; koSf="kqy ksl 'kqfoJ qk AA

(*Mahābhārata, Śalyaparva*, 43.50; 51)

Sarasvatī provided way to Śiva in his compaign to Tripurdāha.

d eZLkR, ar i ksFkZp fofgr kLr = j'e; %
vf/k'Bkuae uLRok lR fjjF, al jLorh AA

(*Mahābhārata, Karṇa Parva*, 5.75)

Mahābhārata Vanaparva (80.118) locates Vinśana in the desert.

Rr ksfou'kuaxPNsfUu; r ksfu; r k'ku%A
XPNR;Ur fgZk; = e#Ik'Bsl j Lor hAA

Mahābhārata Mentions the disappearance of Sarasvatī close to the country of Abhiras, Śudras and Niṣādas.

Rr ksfou'kuaj kt Uk xke gyk;qk%A
'kwækHkhj ku~i fr }s"kkr~ = u"Vk l j Lor hAA

(*Mahābhārata, Śalyaparva*, 36.1)

Vinaśama is located at boundary of the state of Niṣādas.

, r n~fou'kuauke l j LoR;k fo'kkEi r sA
}kj afu"kknj k"VL; ;Skka}s"kkRl j Lor h
i fo"Vk i Foha oh j ek fu"kkn fg ekafon%AA

During *Rāmāyaṇa* period *Āgneyī* used to flow near Ailadhana or Modern Elanabad in Fatehabad Dist. of Haryana.

, y/kkusunhar hRokZi k; pki j i oZku A
f'kyeka dqZhar hRokZv kXus; ha' 'kY; d 'kZksAA

(*Rāmāyaṇa*, 1962 : Vol.ii, *Ayodhyā Kāṇḍa*, 62.10 ff.)

Mahābhārata Describes Sarasvatī named seven river

jkt u~l Ir l j LoR;ks; kfHkO;kIr fenat xr~

(*Mahābhārata Śalyaparva*, 38.3)

Plakṣa Prasravaṇa has been described as the origin of Sarasvatī

i Hkoap l j LoR;k%Iy {ki z o.kacy%

(*ibid.* 54.11)

Sarasvatī's confluence with the western sea.

Lkeqnai f'peaxRok l j LoR;fCk l xee~A

17.2 References of Sarasvatī in *Purāṇas*

Hkweafonk; Zr L; kk/dko'Vk xt xkeuh A
r nUr/kkZekxZki ØÙk i f'pekfHkeq[kh AA

(*Skanda Purāṇa*,1.35.26)

l j Lor; kafou'kusIy {ki z ø. ksr Hk A
Qyk r Hkzn"knoR; kaf=Iy {ksp fo'kkr %

(*Brahmāṇḍa Purāṇa*, 2.3)

Iy {ko{kkr Lr eqHkwrk l fj PN"Bk l ukruh A
LkoZki {k; dj h Lej.kknso fuR; 'k%AA
r= nsoknn'kkFk i q; kai ki foekspuhe~
Iy {kt kacge. k%i eq[kagfj ft gokal j Lor he~AA

(*Vāmana Purāṇa*, 42.7&23.13)

Sarasvati and Ganga have been used as a common name for all rivers.

l okZ i q; k%l j LoR; %l okZ xaxk%l eqxk%

(*Mārkaṇḍeya Purāṇa*, 57.30)

, oeqDRok rnk r su cge.kk p l j Lor h A
fgeoUr afxfj ai kI; fi Ii y knkJ ekÙkuk AA
r Lek r~LFkkukÙkr ksnsohi zIP; fHkeq[ka; ; kS A
vUr/kkZu l ki kIr k dnsk; fgee/; xe~
rR lyk{ fxj s%J x dnskjL; i q%dLFkr %A
r sukfXuk dj LFkS ng;~ekuk l j Lor h AA
r L; kk%HkeaFkwafonk; Zi fo"Vk xt xkeuh A
r nUr/kkZekxZki ØÙk i f'pekfHkeq[kh AA

(*Skanda Purāṇa, Prabhāsa Khaṇḍa*,1.35.21 and 24-26)

LukRok 'kq) eokIukfr ; = i kph l j Lor h
nsekxZk i fr "Bk ; knsekxZk fu%or k AA
vFkkn{kr jkt kr qg; eKk'kr s u l %A
cgekor Zeuk%{ks=s; = i kph l j Lor h AA
i q)dj kj.; ekl k{ i kph ; = l j Lor h A
efr %Lefr % 'kq)k i z k AA

r= nshann' kkZk i q; kai k foekspuhe~A
ly{kt kacge.k%i eqhagfj ft gokal j Lor he~AA
(*Vāmana Purāṇa*, 23.13)

Yk{eh%d j Lor h xak fr l kslHk; kZgj \$fi A
Ikk.kk l ekLr kfLr 'Bfir l r r agfj l fu/kkSAA
(*Devī Bhāgvata Purāṇa*, 2.9.6.17)

IkoZunh ai fr r kegs l "Vk l eaHkwx. kS%d eLr SA
(*Vāmana Purāṇa*, 23.44)

Lkekgyw r r ksnshaLokal qkai ne l Hkb%
mokp i qf= xPN Roax gRokfXuaegksf/ke~AA
(*Skanda Purāṇa, Prabhāsa khaṇḍa*, 17.53)

Sarasvatī's merging with Gaṅgā and its identification as the eastern flow or Prācī Sarasvatī.

Ikq; {ks=sá kt xke Hkkjr sl k l j Lor h
Xkak'kksu dy; k Lo; ar LFkkSgj \$%i ne~AA
(*Brahmvaivarta Purāṇa*, 2.7.1

, oeqRok l foi f'kZor h Z/kj kr y sA
xr %dy {kr ea; Leknor h kkZl j Lor h AA
l ekf/kar= l ák; fufo"Vks/kj . khr y sA
l Hkkai j eaxRok fo'ofe=L; pkisfj AA
(*Skanda Purāṇa, Nāgar khaṇḍa*, 173.)

Sarasvatī originated piercing the earth.

j Uk\$; su foi kbnk y kspuk\$Ikafuj h{k kkr ~A
, dL; l fyyaf{ki z; = t kr k l j Lor h AA
(*Skanda Purāṇa, Nāgara khaṇḍa*, 12.)

According to *Bhāgavata Purāṇa* (1.9.1) Bhiṣma had fallen in Vinaśana.

bfr Hkhr %i z kn kgk r ~l oZe Zfofr R ; kA
r r ksfou'kuai kxkRk; = noozkisi r r ~AA

Balarāma is also mentioned to have gone to Vinaśana to forestall the mace duel between Bhima and Duryodhana.

l %Hkhenq kZku; kx Zkh\$Ika; q r ks ZksA

okf; "; u~fou'kuat xke ; nqLrju AA

Viśvāmitra cursed Sarasvatī to get mixed up with blood, on account of her failure to deliver Ṛṣi Vasiṣṭha to him.

r r %d j Lor h ' 'klr k fo'okfe=sk /khe r k A
v gPNkf kr kfle J ar kş al øR j ar nk AA

Skanda Purāṇa, *Nāga*ra *Khaṇḍa* 173.9-14, refers to the birth of the Prācī Sarasvatī and the Sāmbhramatī at the same time as a result of seismic-tectonic upheaval close to the source of Sarasvatī.

, oeqRok l foi f'kyor h Z/kj kr y sA
xr %dy {kr #a; Lekn or h kkZ j Lor h
l ekf/kar = l ákk; fufo"Vks/kj . khr y sA
l ãkeai j eaxRok fo'okfe=L; pkisfj
ok#.ks eæsk oh{k; Ldl ékkr y e~A
r r ksfufHkZ ol ékaHkÿr kş afofuxZe~A
j ákş; s foi kok y kpukH; kafuj h{k kkr ~A
, d L; Lkfy y af{ki a; = t kr k l j Lor h A
ly {key sr r Lr L; oxski âr scy kr ~A
r nZ ar s l E ykZr r Lr s egkunh A
f}r h Lr qi zkgks; %d ãkekÙk; fuxZ%A
l kp l kHkr h uke unh t kr k/kj kr y sA

Disappearance of Sarasvatī after the formation of Himalayas is described in *Padma Purāṇa* (*Sṛṣṭi Khaṇḍa*, 18.198), as

l kr axgRok l dq kskh i zkP; fHkeq[ka; ; kSA
v Ur/kkZu s l akkr k i ¢dj al k egkunh AA

The sea was present till Bhādrā near Nohar in Rajasthan. This fact has been verified by an episode in *Mahābhārata* in which the sage Utatthya drinks off the entire water of the ocean on Varuṇa's refusal to return his bride Bhadrā whom the Gods have forcibly abducted. This country is reduced to a desert and Utatthya asks the Sarasvatī to go invisible into it so that, forsaken by her, it becomes inauspicious.

Ukkj nL; op%J¥RoK Ø¼q % LkToy nx~kj kA
vfi cUÙkk l k okfj fo'kh; l qgkr i k%AA

(*Anuśāsana Parva*,139.22)

Rkr Lr nhfj . kat kr al eq¾pki l fiZ%A
RkLeknn`'kkUnhap S i kslpk kSf}t kÙke%AA
vn'; kxPN Hkh# Roal jLofr e#ai fr A
vi q; , 'kHkor qn`'kLR; D Lro; k' 'kqHkAA

Tradition of *Skanda Purāṇa* (1.35.26) also points out the fact that mighty Sarasvatī pierced the earth's crust and started flowing westward invisibly.

Hkkafonk; Zr L; k/k%i fo"Vk xt xkfeuh A
RknUr/kkZekxZk i oÙk i f'pekfHkeq[kh AA

As per tradition of *Skanda Purāṇa* (7.33.40-41), Sarasvatī descended on the earth through *Plakṣa.*

Lkr hfol T; r kanohaunh HkRok l j Lor h A
fgeoUr afxfj ai kM; Ly {kkr ~r = fofuxZk AA
vor h kkZ/kj ki 'Bs———

As per tradition of Harivaṁśa Purāṇa (46.29-52) seaward flowing Yamunā changed its course during *Mahābhārata* Period as per wishes of Balarāma.

l eÙkkscfy ukaJ s'Bkst k%kfv/kZkuu%A
'kS kj h'kqf=; kek q; Hkk Losky l %'k%kh AA
cyj keLr q; equkek g Lukr q¶ PNseghunh A
, fg ekfeeaxPN Roa: fi . kh l kxj xesA

17.3 References of Sarasvatī in Śrauta Sūtras

vXu; sdkek; f'V%dy {ksi kl ø. ksA

(*Kātyāyana Śrauta Sūtra*, 1972, 24.7.7)

voHkFkeH;o; fUr ; equkad kj i poai fr A

(*Ibid.* 24.7.10)

According to the commentator:

d kj i poksnš kfo'kk"k r Ue/; s; equk or ZsA
ukoHkFkal j LoR; keA

(*Ibid.* 24.7.22.)

; nk Iy {ka i kl ø. kekxPNfUr vFkkoHkkufefr Iy {ka
i kl ø. kekxE; i qjLr knfr j k=L; kXu; s d kek; f'V%
L; kfnfr ' 'kkf. MY; %A

(*Lāṭyāyana Śr. Sū.* 10.17.12-14).

vFk l kj Lor kfuA l j LoR; k%i f'pes mnd kUr s nh{ksuA
r sr =S nh{kks l n%d Rok i k; . kh; ap l j Lor hanf{k.ksu
r hjsk 'kE; ki kl s vgj g; Zekuk vuqz ;q%A
vFkkoHkkukfuA Iy k{kai z ø. kai kl ; koHkuEkA ; s ; equk; ka
d kj i posoHkFkeH;qs q%A

(*Āśvalāyana Śrauta Sūtra*, 1917: PP. 443.)

vFk l kj Lor kfu l j LoR; k mnd kUr snh{ksu~A

(*Āśvlāyana Śrauta Sūtra*, 1917 : 6.6.1)

'kq"y i {k Ir E; kanh{kk l j Lor h fou'kus——

(*Kātyāyana Śrauta Sūtra*, 1972 : 24.5.30)

Baudhāyana Dharma Sūtra (1.2.10) describes Āryavartta as the country lying to the east of Adarśana (*Vinaśana*), west of Kālakavana, south of Himalayas and north of Pariyātra.

i kxn'kZuk~i R; d kyd oukr~nf{k.ksu fgeoUr e~mnd~
i kfj ; k=e~, r nk; kZor Z~A

17.4 References of Sarasvatī in the Brāhmaṇas

Describing the sacrificial session on the Sarasvatī, the *Pañcaviṁśa Brāhmaṇa (Tāṇḍya Mahābrāhmaṇa*, 936) says:

Lkj LoR;k fou'kusnh{kUrs
Ikzhi a; fUr u á Ldhi e"V oki uxZk Iy {k; k ; fUr
(25.10.12)

Pkr qpRokfj àknk'ohukfu l j LoR;k fou'kukr~ Iy {k%
i Lk o. k%r kofnr % LoxkZ y kd %l j Lorh l fEer s
v/ouk LoxZy kd a; fUr A (25.10.16)

; nk Iy {kai Lk o. kavkxPNUR; FkksRFkkue~A (25.10.21)

d kji poai fr ; equkeoHkFkeH;o; fUr A (25.10.23)

Ṣaḍrātra sacrifice on the southern banks of Sarasvatī

vFkSs 'kMjk=k%A e#r ks ok vd kE; Ur kS 'Bk cfy 'Bk
Hkfy 'Bk oh; ZÙk ek nokuke~L; ke(t ; s LoxZ kd abfr A
r ,r a 'kMjk=a ; Ke~ vi '; uA—r sakt ; Ur A r Ska
l j LoR; k mi eTt us nh{kkA nf{k ks r hjs nh{kUrsA
l j LoR; k ; fUr A okx~oSl j Lor h A okx~m ns; ku%
i UFkk%A ns; kusuS r RFkk ; fUr A i zhi a; fUr A i zhi
bo oS LoxkZy kd %A LoxZ~, o r Yy kd ai fr i| UrsA
i kp mnp ; fUr A i k³ ~bo g ok bna LoxkZy kd %A
LoxZ~, o r Yy kd aj kgUrks; fUr A vk i {kkr~i Lk o. kkn~
; fUr A, 'k m g oS okpksUrks; r~i {k%i Lk o. k%A ; =ks
oS okpksUrl ~, rr~LoxkZy kd %A LoxZ, o r Yy kd a
xPNfUr A

(*Jaiminīya Brāhmaṇa*, 2.297-98.)

Small distance to the north of Plakṣa Prāsravaṇa is the centre of Earth. This fact helps in determining the date of Sarasvatī when it used to originate from the Plakṣa. The tradition of *Jaiminīya Up. Br.* (1921: 4.26.18: P. 152) clearly indicates the fact that during that period equator passed through the Plakṣa region of this country. Now the

Plakṣa region of Indian continent has drifted towards 30 degrees north of the equator. As per modern researches of Geology, Indian continent is drifting towards the north at the rate of 2 cms. per year. If the total period of 30 degrees of drift is calculated on the above basis, it comes about more than 16 crore years. The present author has already observed that Plakṣa Sarasvatī belongs to the post-Saṁhitā period or the Brāhmaṇic period, which has been named by the author as glaciation period or pre-Himalayan period. The glacial period goes as far back as 20 crore years ago. The present evidence of the tradition of *Jaiminīya Up. Br.* not only supports the present author,s hypothesis but also helps determine the period of Brāhmaṇic traditions around twenty crore years ago.

ly{kL; i¢k z.kL; i¢nšek=knq~rr~i fFkQSe/; e~
vFk; =Ssl Ir''kZ%r fÌokse/; e~A

(*Jaiminīya Up. Br.*: 4.26.18 : P.152.)

_''k; ks ok l jLoR; ka l =ek l r rs do'ke§'ka
l kekuu; u~nkL; k%i q=%fd r oksckge.k%d Fkauks e/; s
nhf{k'Vkfr ra cfgZkBokogu~ v=Sa fii kl k gUrq
l j LoR; k mnd aek i kfnfr ——

(*Aitareya Brāhmaṇa, 2.19*)

According to *Śatpatha Brāhmaṇa* (2.25.10.1), *Vinaśana* is a place of consecration (*dikṣā*) for Sārasvata and Dārṣadvata (*Yajña*) sessions.

Lkj LoR; k fou'kusnh{kUr s—

Skanda Purāṇa (Nirṇayasāgar Press, *Nāga*ra *Khaṇḍa*, 164.39) appears to state that the flow of the river Sarasvatī went underground after it reached Puṣkarāraṇya (present day Pohkaraṇa near Jind in Harayana) in her tendency to move towards west. So it is crystal clear from this reference that Vinaśana is located in Haryana itself and not in Rajasthan.

i q̈dj kj.; ek l k¦ i qLr LekR j Lor h A
vUr) kZaxr k xUrq i zÙk i f'pekeq[kh AA

According to *Pañcvimśa Brāhmaṇa* (25.10) any one undertaking a Sārasvata sacrificial session got initiated at *Vinaśana*.

I j LoR; k fou'kusnh{kUrsA (1)
i zhi a; fUr u á Uohi e"V oSi wZk Ik{kI k; fUr A (12)
n'k} R; k vI; ; si ksai =h; ap#afu# I; kFkk; fUr A (15)
; n Iy {kai kI z. kavkxPNUR; FkkRFkkuaA (21)
d kj i poai fr ; equkeoHkFkEo; fUr A (23)

17.5 References of Sarasvatī in the Vedas

RV (7.95.2) describes Sarasvatī rushing down from clouds to sea.

,dkpsr~ljLorhunhuka' 'kqph;Z
fxfjH; vkleqnzkr~A
jk;'psrUrhHkqZuL; Hkwsj?ksZralk;ksnqgsukgqk; A

Sarasvatī flows like that of sea:

;L; kvuUrksv°#rLRos"k'pfj".kq.kZ%A
ve'pjfr jksf#or~AA

(*RV.* 6.61.8)

iz{kksnl k/kk;l kl l zl jLorh/k#.kek;l hi%A
izokok/kkukjF; s ;kfr fo'okvi kefguk fl U/kqjU;k%

(*RV.* 7.95.1)

Sarasvatī is also called seventh in number and mother of rivers.

vk;r~ lkda ;'kk ks oko'kkuk% l jLorh l IrFkh
fl U/kqekrk

(*RV.* 7.36.6)

Sarasvatī has been described as the best of the rivers, the best of deities, best of mothers.

vfEcr esunhr esnsoh esl jLorh A
vi źkLr kbo Lefl i źkLr heEc uLd f/k AA

(*RV.* 2.41.16)

In the *RV.* 8.54.4, Sarasvatī is invoked separately with seven rivers.

i Vk fo".kqgZuaesl jLoR;oUrql Irfl U/ko%A
vki ksokr %i oZrk ksouLi fr %Ük ks qlkfHkoh goe~AA

In *RV.* (6.61.10; 12) Sarasvatī is refered to as a group of seven rivers.

mr u%fi zkk fi zk ql Ir Lol kl tq"Vk A
l jLorh Lr ks"; kHkw A

f='kkLFkk l Ir /kkr ¶ģ pt kr k o/kZfUr A
okt sokt sgO;kHkw AA

The first time we find the mention of Sarasvatī along with Dṛṣdvatī and Āpayā in *RV.* 3.23.4

n'k} R̦ kaeku¦k vki ; k̦ kal j LoR̦ kaj onXusfnnhfg A

Sarasvatī is also invoked with Yamunā, Sutlej, Gaṅgā and Rāvi in later part of *RV.*10.75.5.

beaesxxs; eqsl j Lor h 'kr qnz Ir ksal pr k
Ik#".; k A

Select Bibliography

1. *Abhidhānacintāmaṇī* of Hemacandra.
2. *Agni Purāṇa*, 1900: Eng. tr. M. N. Dutt.
3. Ali, S.M. 1942: *The problem of desiccation of the Ghaggar plains. Calcutta Geographical Review*, 4, 1
4. Ali, S.M. 1966 (reprinted 1973): *Geography of Purāṇās.* People's Publishing House, New Delhi.
5. Arya, Ravi Prakash. 1995: *Vedic Meteorology*, Parimal Publications, New Delhi.
6. Arya, Ravi Prakash. 1996: *The Sāmaveda Saṁhitā*, Parimal Publications, New Delhi.
7. Arya, Ravi Prakash. 1996 *The Yajurveda Saṁhitā*, Parimal Publications, New Delhi.
8. Arya, Ravi Prakash. 1997: *The Ṛgveda Saṁhitā*, 4 Vols. Parimal Publications, New Delhi.
9. Arya, Ravi Prakash. 1998: *The Rāmāyaṇa*, 4 Vols. Parimal Publications, New Delhi.
10. Arya, Ravi Prakash. 1998: *The Yogavasiṣṭha*, 4 Vols. Parimal Publications, New Delhi.
11. Allchin, B., Goudie, A., and Hegde, K. 1978: *The Prehistory and Palaeography of the Great indian Desert.* Academic Press, London.
12. *Āśvalāyana Śrauta Sūtra* (*ASS*), 1917: Anandasrama Series, ed. S.R. Gokhale, Poona.
13. *Bhāgavat Purāṇa* : Bangabashi Office, Calcutta.
14. Bhargava, M.L. 1964: *The Geography of Ṛgvedic India*, Lucknow.
15. *Bhaviṣya Purāṇa*: Bangabashi Office, Calcutta.

16. *Brahma Purāṇa*: Bangabashi Office, Calcutta.

17. *Brahmavaivarta Purāṇa,*.Bangabashi Office, Calcutta.

18. *Brahmāṇḍa Purāṇa*

19. Bargess, J. 1885: On the Identification of places in Sanskrit Geography of India, quoted by S.M. Ali, 1966.

20. *Bṛhannāradīya Purāṇa*, Gita Prass Gorakhpur.

21. *Devi Bhāgvat Purāṇa*, Gita Press Gorakhpur.

22. Dey, N.L. 1921: The early Course of Ganges, quoted by S.M. Ali, 1966.

23. Dey N.L. 1927 (reprinted 1979): *The Geographical Dictionary of Ancient and Mediaeval India.* Cosmo Publications, New Delhi.

24. Dwivedi, R.K. 1975: *The Saraswati Complex in Mahābhārata*, pub. K.C. Chattopadhyaya Memorial Vol., Allahabad.

25. *Garuḍa Purāṇa*, Bangabashi Office, Calcutta.

26. Gazetteer of Ambala District, 1892, Lahore.

27. *Geography of Mahābhārata.*

28. *Geographical Horizon of Mahābhārata.*

29. Ghose, B., Kar, Amal and Hussain, Zahid 1978: *Comparative Role of Aravalli and Himalayan river systems in the fluvial sedimentation of the Rajasthan desert.* A paper presented at the symposium on Tertiary and Quarternary Climatic and Environmental Changes, Tenth International Congress of Anthropological and Ethnological Sciences, December 1978.

30. Godbole, N.N. 1963: *Rigvedic Saraswati*, Jaipur.

31. *Harivaṁśa Purāṇa*, Gita Press Gorakhpur.

32. Hazra, R.C.1937:*Padma Purāṇa*, Indian Culture Vol. 4

33. *Indian Antiquary*: 1932.

34. *Jain Ādi Purāṇa*

35. *Jaiminīya Brāhmaṇa*, 1954: Ed. Raghuvir, Nagpur.

36. *Jaiminīya Up. Br.*, 1921: Ed. Pt. Ram Deva, Lahore.

37. Indhas, 1967: *Lost Saraswati*, Vallabh Vidyanagar.

38. *Katyāyaṇa Śrauta Sūtra* (KSS) 1972 : Ed. Weber, Chaukhamba, Benaras.

39. Kane, P.V. 1941: *History of Dharmaśāstra*, Poona.

40. *Kāvyamimāṁsā* of Rajashekhar, G.O.S. Ed. Baroda.

41. Krishan M.S.1960: *Geology of India and Burma*. Higginbothams, Madras.

42. Kṛtya Kalpataru of Bhaṭa Laxmidhar, 1942 Ed. KV Rangaswami Aiyangar, GOS, Baroda.

43. *Kūrma Purāṇa*, Bangabashi Office, Calcutta.

44. Lal, B.C : *Rivers of India*, Calcutta.

45. *Lāṭyāyana Śrauta Sūtra* (*LSS*), 1872: Edited by Ānandacandra Vedāntavāgīśa. Bibliotheca Indica, Calcutta.

46. Majumdar, R.C. 1965: *The Vedic Age*, London.

47. *Matsya Purāṇa*, Bangabashi Office, Calcutta.

48. *Mahābhārata,* Bangabashi Press, Calcutta.

49. *Mahābhaṣya* of Patañjali, Rohtak.

50. *Manusmriti.*, J.P. Publications, Delhi

51. *Mārkaṇḍeya Purāṇa*, Bangabashi Office, Calcutta.

52. Mughal, M. Rafique 1979: *New Archeological Evidence from Bhawalpur*. A paper presented at the International Seminar on Indus Valley Civilization at Karachi.

53. *Nirukta* of Yāska, Sanskrit Tr. by Brahma Muni Privrajaka.

54. Oldham, C.F. 1893: *The Saraswati and the lost river of*

the Indian desert. Journal of Royal Asiatic Society (N.S.) 34:49-76.

55. Ojha, Gauri Shankar Hira Chand, 1954: *Ojha Nibandha Sangrah*, Udaipur.

56. *Pañcaviṁśa Brāhmaṇa*, 1870: Ed. Ananda Chandra, Calcutta.

57. Sankrityayana, Rahul 1957: *Ṛgvedic Arya*, Allahabad.

58. *Rāmāyaṇa* of Vālmīki, 1962: Baroda.

59. *Rāmāyaṇa* of Vālmīki, Gujrati Press edition.

60. Rayachaudhuri, C. 1958: *Studies in Indian Antiquities.* Calcutta.

61. Rayachaudhuri, H.C. 1972: *Political History of Ancient India*, Calcutta.

62. Saxena, 1976: *Regional Geography of Vedic India*, Kanpur.

63. Sircar, D.C. 1971: Studies in the Geography of Ancient and Mediaeval India. 3rd edition, Delhi.

64. *Skanda Purāṇa*, Nag publication, Delhi.

65. Stein, A.1942: *A Survey of Ancient Sites along the 'lost' Saraswati river.* Geographical Journal, 99:173-82.

66. *Tāṇḍya Brāhamaṇa* 1936: Benaras.

67. Vaidya C.V. *History of Vedic Literature.*

68. Vaidya, P.L. 1962: *Rāmāyaṇa*, Baroda.

69. *Vāmana Purāṇa*, 1893: Ed. M. C. Pal, Calcutta.

70. *Vāyu Purāṇa*, Bangabashi Office, Calcutta.

71. *Viṣṇu Purāṇa*, Tr. Wilson, H.H

72. Wadia, D. N. 1975 (reprint 1976): *Geology of India.* Tata-McGraw-Hill, New Delhi.

73. Wilhelmy, H. 1969: *Das Urstromtal am Ostrand der indusebene und der Saraswati-Problem. Zeitschrift für Geomorphologie*, Supp.8: 76-93.

www.ingramcontent.com/pod-product-compliance
Lightning Source LLC
Chambersburg PA
CBHW021133020426
42331CB00005B/746
* 9 7 8 8 1 8 7 7 1 0 6 9 1 *